Gems &
Minerals

O F   T H E   S O U T H W E S T

Gems &
Minerals
OF THE SOUTHWEST

JENNIFER SANO

PHOTOGRAPHY BY JEFFREY A. SCOVIL

RIO NUEVO PUBLISHERS
TUCSON, ARIZONA

Rio Nuevo Publishers®
P.O. Box 5250, Tucson, Arizona 85703-0250
(520) 623-9558, www.rionuevo.com

Shown on the front cover: cinnabar. On the back cover (left to right): elbaite, gypsum, chrysocolla. On page 2: antlerite; page 6: muscovite and albite; page 9: cuprite; page 10: wulfenite; page 87: sphalerite and sidarite; page 90: chalcocite; page 93: linarite; page 96: cinnabar.

Library of Congress Cataloging-in-Publication Data

Sano, Jennifer.
  Gems and minerals of the Southwest / Jennifer Sano ; photography by Jeffrey A. Scovil.
    p. cm.
  ISBN 978-1-933855-23-3
  1. Minerals—Southwestern States. 2. Gems—Southwestern States. 3. Mineralogy—Southwestern States. I. Scovil, Jeffrey A. II. Title.
  QE375.5.S97S26 2008
  549.979—dc22
                        2008006831

Design: Dawn D. Sokol, D. Design Studio, Tempe, AZ
Cover design: Karen Schober, Seattle, Washington

Printed in Korea.

10 9 8 7 6 5 4 3 2 1

CONTENTS

ABOUT THIS BOOK

This book provides an enjoyable and informative look at some of the minerals found in the southwestern area of the United States. It is intended to be a resource for budding rock enthusiasts who want to identify gems and minerals spotted along a hiking trail or in a collection at home, or simply to learn more about the Southwest's unique natural resources. The minerals included here are a comprehensive but by no means complete list of the vast mineral resources of the Southwest. Those described here were chosen for their importance as basic rock-forming minerals or for their prevalence throughout or uniqueness to the Southwest—such as turquoise or red beryl, respectively—or for some interesting cultural ties to the region, such as Apache tears. The mineral descriptions include photographs and are organized alphabetically by name unless they appear as part of a group such as feldspar, garnet, mica, olivine, tourmaline, or zeolite, wherein related minerals have the same general formula but with some substitutions among the elements. Keep in mind that many of the photographs are of pristine specimens of the described minerals and are not always representative of how they look in the field. The descriptions provide an idea of what the mineral would look like in its natural environment.

Some terms commonly used by geologists appear in **boldface;** most of these are defined in the glossary or near where they first appear in the text.

THE GEOLOGIC SETTING

The Southwest is an area rich in mineral resources born from an active geologic past. The term "Southwest" for the purposes of this book refers to Nevada, southeastern California, Arizona, New Mexico, southwestern Colorado, southern Utah, and western Texas. More accurately in terms of geology, it refers mainly to the Basin and Range Province, the Colorado Plateau, and a small part of the southwestern Great Plains.

The Great Plains and the Colorado Plateau, in contrast to the Basin and Range Province, have experienced only minor adjustments in their geologic past, most recently undergoing regional **tectonic** uplift. The lowermost—or basement—rock in this area consists of **igneous** and **metamorphic** material that became part of the older North American **craton** between 1.8 and 1.6 billion years ago. Younger igneous rocks (between 1 and 1.4 billion years old) visible in the region formed by forcing their way through the basement rock as hot **magma** from below, and as such are called igneous intrusions. Over millions of years, the rocks have been eroded, covered by sediment, eroded, and covered again, leaving the variety of **sedimentary** rocks that the area is famous for.

Much of the landscape we see in the Southwest today is the result of changes in **lithospheric plate** motion that began 30 million years ago when the Pacific-Farallon Plate was being **subducted** beneath the westward-moving North American Plate. This process allowed material from the deeper **mantle** to rise up, causing melting and increased **magmatism** with extensive volcanic eruptions. By about 20 million years ago, the entire Farallon Plate, along with its **spreading center,** was completely overlain by the North American Plate. The spreading center, known as the East Pacific Rise, continued to stretch and spread hot magma along the underside of the North American Plate. This heating and spreading allowed the region to stretch like taffy. Some areas stretched enough to break into huge mountain blocks that partially rotated, as books on a shelf do when a bookend is removed. The higher mountainous areas eroded, filling the lower areas with sediment. This is what formed the mountains and sediment-filled valleys of the Basin and Range Province, and this process is still going on.

These events gave the Southwest its unique geological character, and thes same processes will continue to reshape the area for millions of years to come.

INTRODUCTION

Rocks and minerals are all around us, from the countertops in our kitchens to the microchips in our computers. But how often do we stop to consider where these resources come from and how they form? The variety of minerals on this planet is a result of the abundance of particular elements and the geological processes that have occurred over billions of years. To begin understanding minerals, let's first look at rocks.

TYPES OF ROCKS

Rocks are broken down into three categories: igneous, sedimentary, and metamorphic.

Igneous rocks form from the cooling of magma. As the molten material cools, minerals crystallize from the melt. If magma cools slowly, crystals have more time to grow and larger minerals will form. This occurs in rocks that cool below the surface, also called **intrusive rocks.** If magma cools quickly, the minerals may be so small that they're not visible to the naked eye. This occurs in rocks that are erupted, such as from volcanoes, and these are called **extrusive rocks.** The types of minerals that crystallize from magma depend on the chemical composition of the liquid.

Sedimentary rocks form from deposition of a wide range of sediments, which are then compacted and cemented together. The minerals in sedimentary rocks will depend on the minerals in the source rocks.

Metamorphic rocks form when igneous, sedimentary, or other metamorphic rocks are subjected to intense pressure and heat, but not enough to cause complete melting. The minerals that form in metamorphic rocks will depend on the ingredients provided by the parent rock, as well as the degree and duration of elevated pressure and heat.

WHAT ARE MINERALS?

The solid earth is made of rocks, rocks are made of minerals, and minerals are made of elements. More formally, a mineral is a naturally occurring, inorganic solid with a repetitive atomic (or "crystalline") structure and a well-defined chemical composition. Minerals are classified by their chemical composition and atomic structure. Some of the most common rock-forming minerals are quartz, feldspar, and mica, which can be found in all rock types. Other common minerals are amphiboles, pyroxenes, and olivines in igneous rocks; calcite, dolomite, hematite, limonite, halite, and gypsum in sedimentary rocks; and talc, chlorite, garnet, kyanite, sillimanite, andalusite, staurolite, and magnetite in metamorphic rocks.

CHEMICAL COMPOSITION AND CLASS

Minerals are categorized by classes, which are based on their chemical compositions. For example, minerals that are based on the $(SiO_n)^{4-2n}$ **anionic** complex are called silicates (for example, garnet or aquamarine). Silicates are the most common minerals in the earth's crust. Carbonates (such as calcite or azurite) are minerals based on the $(CO_3)^{2-}$ complex, and sulfates (such as gypsum or talc) are based on the $(SO_4)^{2-}$ complex. There are many more mineral classes, but these three are among the most common. The class for each mineral in this book is listed along with the mineral description.

ATOMIC STRUCTURE/CRYSTAL SYSTEM

Despite the tremendous variety of minerals, all of them can be grouped into one of six crystal systems: **cubic (or isometric), tetragonal, hexagonal, orthorhombic, monoclinic,** and **triclinic.** These systems are defined by the lengths and angles of the mineral's axes of symmetry. An in-depth discussion of crystal systems is beyond the scope of this book. However, the crystal system for each mineral is listed for those wishing to explore the subject further. The important thing to realize is that the crystal system is a result of a mineral's atomic structure, and is therefore the same for every specimen of a particular mineral, even though they may look quite different. Also, the atomic structure is what defines the physical properties that help identify a mineral.

PHYSICAL PROPERTIES OF MINERALS

There are many physical properties that can be used to identify a mineral. Some of the most useful ones, as described here, are color, luster, habit (which pertains to shape), cleavage, density, diaphaneity, and hardness. Each mineral in this book has a list of these characteristics.

COLOR: This is the easiest property to notice, and some minerals are recognizable by their color. However, many minerals can take on a variety of colors, so in most cases it is best not to use it as a diagnostic tool.

LUSTER: This refers to the appearance of a mineral in light, or how it reflects light. Common terms to describe luster are:

> *Metallic:* shiny with the appearance of polished metal
> *Submetallic:* has the appearance of dull or weathered metal
> *Nonmetallic:* has any of the following qualities:
>> *Adamantine:* gem-like, sparkling
>> *Earthy or dull:* reflects little light, looks like soil or clay
>> *Greasy:* looks as if it is coated in oil
>> *Pearly:* iridescent; looks like mother-of-pearl
>> *Resinous:* resin-like, looks like dull glass
>> *Silky:* appears to be composed of fine fibers (like silk fabric)
>> *Vitreous:* glassy
>> *Waxy:* having the appearance of wax

HABIT: This term refers to the shape or shapes a mineral will form. A mineral can tend to form individual crystals, crystal aggregates, or both. Habit can be purely descriptive, or it can relate to the mineral's crystal symmetry. Here are some common terms to describe habit:

INDIVIDUAL DISTINCT CRYSTALS
> *Acicular:* needle-like
> *Bladed:* elongated, thin crystals flattened like a knife blade
> *Blocky:* roughly similar dimensions in all directions
> *Equant:* having the same dimensions in all directions, like a box or ball
> *Filiform or capillary:* hair-like
> *Foliated (or micaceous):* easily separated into sheets
> *Prismatic:* elongated crystals with opposite faces parallel to one another
> *Tabular or platy:* having the appearance of stacked sheets; thin tabular would look like a stack of paper, while thick tabular is like a stack of cards

CRYSTAL AGGREGATES
> *Asbestiform or fibrous:* having the appearance of fibers
> *Botryoidal:* having the appearance of a bunch of grapes or bubbles
> *Coating:* covering on the surface of a rock or other mineral
> *Columnar:* parallel columns
> *Cryptocrystalline:* made of grains too small to be seen

Dendritic: branch-like appearance

Drusy: a coating with small, projecting crystals

Globular: made of spherical or hemispherical shapes of radiating crystals

Granular: many individual grains packed together

Massive: solid, dense, no distinguishing characteristics

Radiating: crystals growing outward from a common point

Reniform: forming kidney-shaped nodules

Stalactitic: elongated, having the appearance of thick icicles

Tabular or platy: flat plates growing together

TERMS THAT DESCRIBE HABIT IN RELATION TO CRYSTAL SYMMETRY

Dodecahedron: a form of twelve diamond-shaped faces

Octahedron: a form with eight faces, all shaped as equilateral triangles; looks like two tetrahedrons connected along one face

Rhombohedron: a form with six rhomb-shaped faces (a rhomb is a parallelogram with equal-length sides and interior angles of 60 and 120 degrees)

Scalenohedron: a form of eight or twelve faces shaped like scalene triangles (three unequal sides)

Tetrahedron: a form of four equilateral triangular faces; looks like a pyramid when resting on one face

CLEAVAGE: A repeated fracture along planes of weakness in a mineral's structure is called cleavage. Minerals can cleave in one, two, three, four, or six directions depending on atomic structure. The quality of cleavage is described as perfect, imperfect, distinct, good, fair, or poor, depending on how clean the break is. Cleavage can also be described in terms of crystal symmetry. Cleavage is mentioned in this book only when it is particularly descriptive of a mineral. While it is an important property for mineral identification, it requires a deeper understanding of atomic structure than this book provides.

DENSITY: This is simply the mass of an object divided by its volume. In terms of minerals, it can also be defined by specific gravity, which relates a mineral's density to that of water. This book refers to a mineral's density only when it is particularly characteristic, and it is not quantified. To keep things simple, just remember that if a material feels much lighter than it looks as if it should (for example, pumice), it has a low density, and if it feels much heavier than it looks as if it should (for example, lead) it has a high density.

DIAPHANEITY: This describes a mineral's ability to transmit light.

> *Transparent:* can be seen through
>
> *Translucent:* cannot be seen through, but light passes through
>
> *Opaque:* light does not pass through

HARDNESS: The hardness of a mineral is rated on a relative scale from 1 to 10, with 1 being the softest and 10 being the hardest. The scale, developed by German mineralogist Friedrich Mohs (1773–1839), lists the hardness of particular minerals as well as that of common items. The hardness of all minerals can be understood on a comparative basis. For example, apatite (5) scratches fluorite (4) and is scratched by feldspar (6).

MOHS HARDNESS SCALE

1)	talc
2)	gypsum
2.5)	*fingernail*
3)	calcite
3.5)	*penny*
4)	fluorite
5)	apatite
5.5)	*glass*
6)	feldspar
6.5)	*ceramic plate*
7)	quartz
8)	topaz
9)	corundum
10)	diamond

WHAT IS A GEM?

There are many different definitions of what actually makes a mineral a gem. Some consider only transparent, facetable material a gem. Others use a looser definition that includes opaque minerals such as opal, turquoise, and jade. What makes something a gem is not only its chemical composition, but also its color, clarity, rarity, and the way it reflects light. For example, sapphires and rubies are just the common mineral corundum with uncommon clarity and color. Another important characteristic for a mineral to be used as a gem is that it is durable enough to withstand cutting, polishing, and wearing. This book uses the term *gem* for any material that is commonly faceted or polished for jewelry regardless of its transparency or market value, and uses "precious" and "semiprecious" to further clarify the mineral's value when possible. Other minerals that are commonly polished and used for carving and ornamental purposes other than jewelry are called *lapidary material.* Many of the lapidary materials mentioned in this book are commonly used by the indigenous people of the Southwest for carving fetishes and other ceremonial and ornamental pieces. An excellent book to read for more information about carvings of Southwest Indian artists is *Spirit in the Stone* by Mark Bahti.

A FEW MORE TERMS

You will find a few geologic terms repeated throughout this book. A few of the most common terms are explained here; others are in the glossary at the end.

Many of the minerals described in this book result from **hydrothermal activity,** which means they are the result of processes involving very hot fluids that are associated with **magmatic activity.** The hot fluids may be residual fluids from the magma after much of it has crystallized, or they may be groundwater that has been heated during crystallization of the magma. When these hot fluids pass through and react with other rocks, it is called **hydrothermal alteration,** while **hydrothermal deposit** refers to a mineral deposit that precipitated out of a **hydrothermal fluid.**

Veins are simply fractures in rocks within which minerals have been deposited. Hydrothermal fluids flow easily into these fractures and minerals often precipitate out, forming a **hydrothermal vein deposit**. Most of the copper minerals found in the Southwest occur as **porphyry copper deposits,** which form from magmatic activity that heats and circulates groundwater, as mentioned above. This process leaches copper and other metals from the preexisting rock, and when the water cools, the metals precipitate out and form large deposits.

The term **primary mineral** means that the mineral formed at the same time as the rock in which it is found. **Secondary mineral** refers to a mineral that formed from the alteration of a primary mineral. This alteration can occur by hydrothermal fluids as mentioned above, or by **oxidation** caused by interaction with cold surface water. Oxidation means an atom loses electrons, which allows it to bond with oxygen. For example, iron metal (Fe) can oxidize to form Fe^{3+}, the positive charge resulting from the loss of three electrons. Two of the positively charged iron atoms can then bond with three O^{2-} atoms, forming Fe_2O_3, a.k.a. hematite.

The term **ore** refers to any mineral or rock that can be mined or worked for a profit. **Orebody** refers to the whole body of material to be mined, including the gangue and the ore minerals. **Gangue** refers to the uneconomic portion of that body of material, and the **ore minerals** are the economic minerals in the deposit.

A NOTE ON THE METAPHYSICAL ASPECT
OF GEMS AND MINERALS

Many people are drawn to the use of mineral stones for their reported metaphysical qualities. Some of these symbolic associations come from Native American lore, while others come from European folk traditions that go back several centuries; some of these ideas are found in ancient Greek, Roman, and Egyptian writings, as well as the Bible. Discussing these beliefs in a book called *The Curious Lore of Precious Stones,* gemologist George Frederick Kunz wrote in 1913, "Many of these ideas may seem strange enough to us now, and yet when we analyze them we find that they have their roots either in some intrinsic quality of the stones or else in an instinctive appreciation of their symbolical significance." While *Gems and Minerals of the Southwest* does not pretend to present a comprehensive view of this system of beliefs, it does provide a few representative samples of some of these associations near the end of the individual listings for many of these gems and minerals. For more detailed treatments of this material, see *The Crystal Bible: A Definitive Guide to Crystals,* by Judy Hall; *Love Is in the Earth: A Kaleidoscope of Crystals,* published by Earth-Love Publishing House (Wheat Ridge, Colorado); or Kunz's book mentioned above, which is still in print.

DESCRIPTIONS

ALUNITE

FORMULA:
$KAl_3(SO_4)_2(OH)_6$
CLASS: sulfates
CRYSTAL SYSTEM:
hexagonal
HARDNESS: 4

Although it is relatively rare in most places, alunite occurs in a variety of locations throughout the Southwest. This mineral gets its name from the Latin word *alumen*, and the element aluminum is named after this mineral. It is the potassium, however, that makes alunite useful in the production of fertilizers.

This mineral forms from hydrothermal alteration of potassium-rich rocks, and it varies in color from white to gray to slightly red, with a vitreous to pearly luster and transparent to translucent crystals. Alunite is most commonly found as massive crusts or coatings, but granular, fibrous, and columnar occurrences are also known.

High-grade alunite is found in Piute County, Utah. This mineral also occurs in Mineral, Hinsdale, Custer, and Dolores Counties, Colorado; Nye County, Nevada; and Lassen Volcanic National Park, Shasta County, California.

Commonly found with quartz and other clay minerals.

ANGLESITE

FORMULA: $Pb(SO_4)$
CLASS: sulfates
CRYSTAL SYSTEM:
orthorhombic
HARDNESS: 2.5–3

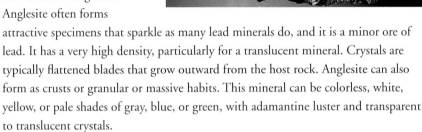

This mineral, named for its
occurrence on the Island of
Anglesey in Wales, forms from
the oxidation of galena.
Anglesite often forms
attractive specimens that sparkle as many lead minerals do, and it is a minor ore of
lead. It has a very high density, particularly for a translucent mineral. Crystals are
typically flattened blades that grow outward from the host rock. Anglesite can also
form as crusts or granular or massive habits. This mineral can be colorless, white,
yellow, or pale shades of gray, blue, or green, with adamantine luster and transparent
to translucent crystals.

Anglesite occurs throughout the Southwest.

*Metaphysical properties: facilitates "channeling" of new information and expression of
spiritual ideas*

Commonly found with galena, cerussite, and barite.

ANHYDRITE

FORMULA: $Ca(SO_4)$
CLASS: sulfates
CRYSTAL SYSTEM: orthorhombic
HARDNESS: 3–3.5

The name comes from the Greek word
anhydrous, meaning "without water,"
which makes sense since it forms when
gypsum ($CaSO_4 \cdot 2(H_2O)$)) loses its
water. Anhydrite is a common mineral
in sedimentary rocks, and it most
commonly forms thick beds along with
evaporites such as halite or calcite. It

can also form as a gangue mineral in hydrothermal ore deposits. This mineral can be colorless, white, bluish white, or lilac, with transparent to translucent crystals and a pearly or vitreous luster. Typical form is granular, fibrous, or massive. Anhydrite can form tabular or prismatic crystals, but they are rare.

Anhydrite is a common lapidary material. *Angelite*, a semitransparent, blue-gray variety of anhydrite, is marketed as a gem. Large anhydrite deposits occur in Eddy County, New Mexico, and Wharton County, Texas.

Metaphysical associations: for accepting unwanted change or differing points of view; dispelling anger

Commonly found with calcite and gypsum.

ANTLERITE

Formula:
$Cu_3(SO_4)(OH)_4$
Class: sulfates
Crystal system:
orthorhombic
Hardness: 3.5–4

Antlerite gets its name from the location where it was first described—the Antler Mine in Mohave County, Arizona. This rare mineral can form as either a primary or secondary mineral in copper ore deposits. In areas where it is abundant, antlerite can be mined as a copper ore mineral. Antlerite is green, white, or gray and has vitreous luster and transparent to translucent crystals. Typical crystal habit is prismatic, but massive antlerite is also common.

In addition to its occurrence at the Antler Mine, antlerite can be found as large crystals at several mines in Cochise County, Arizona. Other occurrences include Coconino and Yavapai Counties, Arizona; Socorro County, New Mexico; Inyo County, California; and Mineral County, Nevada.

Metaphysical associations: facilitates effective coordination between heart and mind
Commonly found with quartz.

APACHE TEARS (OBSIDIAN)

FORMULA, CLASS, AND CRYSTAL SYSTEM: **see description that follows**
HARDNESS: **5–5.5**

These dark-colored, rounded specimens are actually a type of obsidian—a dense volcanic glass of about 70 percent silicon dioxide (SiO_2). Obsidian is not a mineral, as it does not have a crystal structure (and so the formula, class, and crystal system categories don't apply). It is, rather, a mixture of cryptocrystalline silica minerals in a glass-like suspension resulting from quick cooling of silica-rich lava. It is usually found on the edges of lava flows where the lava cools rapidly. The cryptocrystalline minerals are what determine the color, which can range from black to blue, mahogany, or even golden. The presence of magnetite will form black obsidian, whereas hematite will cause a reddish hue.

Obsidian (shown above) can form Apache Tears

Apache Tears are pebble-sized, dark, rounded nodules of obsidian that display smoky-gray translucence when held to the light.

Apache Tears form from weathering of glassy lava domes and are found in several areas of the Southwest. Over time, the volcanic glass alters along fractures to perlite, a soft, gray rock. Portions of glass that are far enough from the fractures will remain unaltered, and the unaffected nodules that are left are called Apache Tears.

One legend of the Apache Tears holds that when the Apaches were under attack, those who were not shot plunged off the edge of a cliff, choosing to take their own lives rather than die at the hands of their enemies. The Apache women and family mourned the loss of their loved ones so deeply that their tears turned into stone.

Arizona supplies the majority of Apache Tears on the market, many coming from perlite mines in the foothills of Apache Leap Mountain in Pinal County.

Metaphysical associations: grounding, protection, healing from grief or negative thoughts

ARAGONITE

FORMULA: $Ca(CO_3)$
CLASS: carbonates
CRYSTAL SYSTEM: orthorhombic
HARDNESS: 3.5–4

Aragonite is a common carbonate mineral and is named for Aragon, Spain, where it was first found. It has the same chemical composition as calcite but a different crystal structure. It is therefore called a **polymorph** of calcite. Aragonite is found in gypsum beds, as hot-spring deposits, or as a precipitate from waters oversaturated with calcium. Many **speleothems** are believed to form as aragonite and change to calcite over time because calcite is the stable form of calcium carbonate at surface pressures and temperatures. Aragonite is usually colorless, white, or pale yellow, with vitreous or resinous luster and transparent to translucent crystals. Typical habit is acicular, prismatic, stalactitic, or fibrous. Aragonite is a common lapidary material.

Large aragonite crystals have been found in Socorro, Chaves, and Guadalupe Counties, New Mexico. This mineral is also found as stalactitic masses in caves throughout the Southwest. Although most of the speleothems in Carlsbad Caverns, New Mexico, are calcite, aragonite formations do occur there.

Metaphysical associations: centering for meditation or to release anger or stress
Commonly found with gypsum, chalcopyrite, and wulfenite.

AURICHALCITE

FORMULA: $(Zn, Cu)_5(CO_3)_2(OH)_6$
CLASS: carbonates
CRYSTAL SYSTEM: monoclinic
HARDNESS: 1–2

The name is a combination of the Latin *aurum* for "gold" and ancient Greek *chalkos* for "copper," in reference to this mineral's zinc and copper composition, not in reference to its color. Aurichalcite is actually a pretty blue to blue-green, as most copper minerals are, and it forms what is best described as a layer of fuzz or moss over rocks. Closer inspection will show small clusters of acicular crystals, sometimes radiating from a center point, that are transparent to translucent with silky luster. Aurichalcite is a secondary mineral that forms from weathering of zinc-copper-sulfide deposits.

Aurichalcite (blue) and hemimorphite

Exceptional specimens of aurichalcite have been found in Cochise, Pima, and Gila Counties, Arizona; Inyo County, Calif.; Socorro County, New Mexico; Juab, Tooele, Washington, and Salt Lake Counties, Utah; and Lake County, Colorado.

Metaphysical associations: releases fear and old patterns of behavior
Commonly found with azurite, malachite, and rosasite.

AZURITE

Formula:
$Cu_3(CO_3)_2(OH)_2$
Class: carbonates
Crystal system: monoclinic
Hardness: 3.5–4

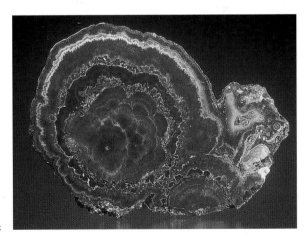

The name comes from the French *azure* in reference to the mineral's color. It is aptly named, as azurite is one of the bluest minerals around. Azurite is a secondary copper mineral that forms from weathering of copper-sulfide rocks. In spite of its uncommon beauty, azurite is fairly common in the Southwest, thanks to the abundance of copper in the area. Most specimens found in the field will be massive crusts with dull luster, but rare transparent to translucent prismatic crystals exist and can rival the beauty of any expensive gemstone. In fact, azurite is commonly used as a semiprecious stone in jewelry, with some of the world's best specimens coming from Bisbee, Arizona.

Azurite is often found along with another copper mineral called malachite (see page 52). This is because further oxidation causes azurite to transform into malachite.

Azurite has been used as a dye for paints and fabrics for centuries. It is a lapidary material, and it is mined as an ore of copper.

Large, nicely formed crystals of azurite can be found in Cochise, Greenlee, Pinal, and Pima Counties, Arizona; Socorro County, New Mexico; and Washington and San Juan Counties, Utah.

Metaphysical associations: enhances creativity; releases worry and hesitation; promotes adaptability

Commonly found with malachite, chalcocite, cuprite, and chrysocolla.

BARITE

Formula: $Ba(SO_4)$
Class: sulfates
Crystal system: orthorhombic
Hardness: 3–3.5

The name barite comes from the Greek word *barys*, meaning "heavy," referring to the mineral's high density. Barite can form as massive deposits, but it is usually when it forms as gangue that nice specimens develop. Usually colorless or white, it can also be blue, yellow, brown, or red. Luster is vitreous to pearly, and crystals are transparent to translucent. Crystal habit is usually thick tabular, but prismatic, lamellar, and granular forms are also possible.

Certain barite specimens form a pattern of blades that look like flower petals. These aggregates are called *barite roses,* or *Cherokee roses* in Oklahoma and Texas.

In addition to being a source of barium for medicinal uses, barite is a weighting agent for oil-well drilling mud and is an additive to cement and automobile paint.

In Colorado, high-quality colorless crystals are found in Mesa County, and blue stones are found in Weld County. Other occurrences include Mineral County, Colorado; Gila County, Arizona; and Elko County, Nevada. Several areas in Nevada produce commercial amounts of barite.

Metaphysical associations: enhances harmony among people; renews intuitive powers; helps release "stuck" emotions

Commonly found with fluorite, galena, quartz, calcite, and dolomite.

BERYL

FORMULA: $Be_3Al_2Si_6O_{18}$
CLASS: silicates
CRYSTAL SYSTEM: hexagonal
HARDNESS: 7.5–8

The name of this mineral comes from the Greek *beryllos*, used as a general term for the blue-green mineral that we now call *aquamarine*, the birthstone for March and Colorado's state gem. But beryl goes by several other names as well: *Emerald*, the green variety of this mineral, is a popular gem and is May's birthstone, and *morganite* is the pink variety found in California **pegmatites.**

Beryl's popularity as a gemstone stems from its variety of colors, the result of trace amounts of impurities. The green of emerald is the result of small amounts of chrome or

Morganite variety of beryl (pink) with albite

vanadium, the blue of aquamarine is caused by the inclusion of iron, and the pink of morganite is from the inclusion of manganese.

The rarest of all beryls, the red beryl, gets its raspberry color from manganese along with small amounts of iron, chrome, and calcium. Red beryl is found in only three places in the world, all of which are in the Southwest: the Thomas Range and the Wah Wah Mountains in Utah, and the Black Range in New

Mexico. The Ruby Violet Mine in southern Utah's Wah Wah Mountains is the only location where gem-quality red beryl is found.

Regardless of color, beryl commonly forms slender prismatic or columnar habit with vitreous luster and transparent to translucent crystals. It is most often found in granitic rocks, particularly pegmatites, but it can also occur in **schists** and in some ore deposits.

Beryl has been prized for centuries, but not only for its beauty. All beryl was believed to be useful in the treatment of eye damage, and aquamarine, said to come from the treasure chests of mermaids, was believed to be a lucky stone for sailors.

In addition to the occurrences listed above, beryl is found in San Diego County, California; Chaffee County, Colorado; and Cochise County, Arizona.

Metaphysical associations: helps one to "pick one's battles," make good choices, and overcome obstacles to success

Commonly found with quartz, feldspar, muscovite, tourmaline, and topaz.

BIXBYITE

FORMULA: $(Mn,Fe)_2O_3$
CLASS: oxides
CRYSTAL SYSTEM: cubic
HARDNESS: 6–6.5

This rare mineral appeals to collectors for its attractive specimens of small, black, shiny cubes in cavities of contrasting light-colored volcanic rock. The cubic crystals often have striated faces and are never larger than 2 cm on edge. Sometimes the cubes will have modified corners in which the points look as if they were filed down.

In addition to cubes, this mineral can be massive or granular. Bixbyite is opaque with metallic luster.

This mineral is named in honor of Maynard Bixby, a mineral dealer from Salt Lake City, Utah, who provided the first specimens of this mineral.

Bixbyite can be found in Juab County, Utah; Sierra and Catron Counties, New Mexico; and Pinal County, Arizona.

Metaphysical associations: for keen awareness and sensitivity

Commonly found with topaz, spessartine, quartz, beryl, sanidine, and hematite.

BORNITE

FORMULA: Cu_5FeS_4
CLASS: sulfides
CRYSTAL SYSTEM:
orthorhombic
HARDNESS: 3

Named after Ignaz von Born
(1742–1791), a German
mineralogist, bornite is
generally dark brown to black.
Bornite commonly occurs in sulfide veins and as a secondary mineral in enriched
zones of sulfide deposits. It is opaque with bronzy metallic luster. Pseudocubic crystals
are possible, but bornite usually occurs as massive deposits. It is an ore of copper and
is common throughout the Southwest.

When bornite tarnishes, it takes on a blue-violet hue that gives it the name
peacock ore. However, chalcopyrite is also sold as peacock ore.

Large quantities occur in Pinal and Cochise Counties, Arizona, and Gilpin
County, Colorado.

*Metaphysical associations: promotes sense of well-being and seeing the "rightness" of
things as they are*

Commonly found with chalcopyrite, chalcocite, covellite, pyrite, and quartz.

BRUCITE

FORMULA: $Mg(OH)_2$
CLASS: hydroxides
CRYSTAL SYSTEM: hexagonal
HARDNESS: 2.5

Brucite is named for Archibald Bruce
(1777–1818), the early American
mineralogist who first described the
species. This mineral usually occurs in
veins of magnesium-rich rocks and can
also be found in metamorphosed
carbonates. It usually forms broad tabular
crystals, light-green to gray in color, with

vitreous to pearly luster. Fibrous aggregates and foliated masses are also common. Brucite is an important ore of magnesium.

Large deposits occur in Nye County, Nevada, and Riverside County, California.

Commonly found with chlorite in magnesium-rich rocks and calcite, dolomite, and talc in carbonate rocks.

CALCITE

FORMULA: $Ca(CO_3)$
CLASS: **carbonates**
CRYSTAL SYSTEM: **hexagonal**
HARDNESS: **3**

Calcite with cuprite inclusions (giving reddish color)

The name comes from the Latin *calx* for "burnt lime," in reference to its industrial use in the production of lime. Calcite is a very common mineral and is a polymorph of aragonite. It is a major ingredient in rocks such as limestone and marble and is often a component of the cement holding sedimentary rocks together. It is also found as a gangue mineral in hydrothermal vein deposits and in igneous rocks.

A particularly striking form of calcite is as cave formations called speleothems. A spectacular example of this occurs in Carlsbad Caverns, New Mexico. There, as in most occurrences, the speleothems formed as aragonite, then changed to calcite, which is more stable at surface temperature and pressure.

Calcite is commonly white to grey, with transparent individual crystals. More than 300 crystal forms have been identified for calcite, but its most common habits are scalenohedra or rhombohedra, and **twinning** is common. Calcite is also found in massive, fibrous, or granular forms. Calcite is soft and can be scratched by a steel knife blade, and it is easily identified by its effervescent reaction with cold dilute hydrochloric acid or vinegar.

In addition to its use in the production of lime, calcite is also used in cements and mortars, and in the glass and optics industries. During the time of the Roman

Empire, calcite was burned along with volcanic ash to produce durable cement that was used to construct buildings. Calcite is also commonly used as a lapidary material.

Calcite is mined in Pima and Pinal Counties, Arizona.

Metaphysical associations: clears negative energy; dispels hopelessness; calms and declutters the mind

Commonly found with dolomite, fluorite, barite, and pyrite in ore deposits; talc, tremolite, grossular, and quartz in metamorphic rocks; and apatite and orthoclase in igneous rocks.

CALEDONITE

FORMULA:
$Pb_5Cu_2(CO)_3(SO_4)_3(OH)_6$
CLASS: sulfates
CRYSTAL SYSTEM: orthorhombic
HARDNESS: 2.5–3

Caledonite gets its name from the country in which it was first found, Scotland, historically known as Caledonia. It is a somewhat uncommon secondary mineral that forms in the oxidized portions of lead-copper deposits. Caledonite is most often blue, blue-green, or dark green with vitreous to resinous luster and transparent to translucent crystals. Habit is most commonly acicular or radiating aggregates, but this mineral can form slender prisms. Nicely formed crystals of transparent blue are attractive but too soft to be used as a gemstone. Large masses of caledonite have been found in Pinal and Maricopa Counties, Arizona; Socorro County, New Mexico; and Beaver Creek, Utah. It also occurs in Inyo and San Bernardino Counties, California; Doña Ana County, New Mexico; and Clear Creek, Gilpin, and Lake Counties, Colorado.

Metaphysical associations: promotes intuition and easy communication of resulting insights

Commonly found with cerussite, malachite, and anglesite.

CARNOTITE
FORMULA: $K_2(UO_2)_2(VO_4)_2 \cdot 3(H_2O)$
CLASS: **vanadates**
CRYSTAL SYSTEM: **monoclinic**
HARDNESS: 1

This mineral is named for Marie-Adolphe Carnot (1839–1920), a French mining engineer and chemist. Carnotite forms as a secondary mineral in uranium deposits hosted in sandstone or conglomerate (a rock formed from large pieces of other rock). It is a bright-yellow mineral with a pearly to dull luster and translucent to opaque crystals. This mineral usually forms as a crust or crumbled aggregates, looking like yellow powder. Carnotite is an important ore of uranium and is radioactive.

Carnotite was first described from deposits in Uravan District, Montrose County, Colorado, but it can be found in many locations throughout Arizona, Colorado, Nevada, New Mexico, and Utah. It occurs as an ore mineral in Apache and Navajo Counties, Arizona. Other occurrences include Mesa and San Miguel Counties, Colorado; Emery and Grand Counties, Utah; and McKinley County, New Mexico.

Metaphysical associations: acceptance and integration of all parts of the self
Commonly found with other uranium-vanadium oxides, gypsum, and barite.

CERUSSITE
FORMULA: $Pb(CO_3)$
CLASS: **carbonates**
CRYSTAL SYSTEM: **orthorhombic**
HARDNESS: 3–3.5

The name comes from the Latin *cerussa,* meaning "white lead." The lead gives this mineral some sparkle, and its tendency to form twinned minerals results in some attractive specimens. Typical habit is tabular or prismatic, but it is common for cerussite to develop three intersecting prisms, or "sixling twins," forming a starburst shape. Cerussite is usually colorless to white, with transparent to translucent crystals and adamantine luster. Acicular, granular, and massive habits are also possible. One distinguishing characteristic is cerussite's tendency to effervesce in cold dilute hydrochloric acid.

Cerussite forms in the oxidized zone of lead-sulfide ore deposits. Up until the 1920s, cerussite was a major source of lead.

Occurrences include Lake County, Colorado; Pinal and Santa Cruz Counties, Arizona; and Dona Ana County, New Mexico.

Metaphysical associations: for feeling "at ease" away from home; facilitates adaptability/adjustment and ability to move forward in life

Commonly found with galena, anglesite, malachite, and azurite.

CHALCANTHITE

FORMULA: $Cu(SO_4) \cdot 5(H_2O)$
CLASS: **sulfates**
CRYSTAL SYSTEM: **triclinic**
HARDNESS: **2.5**

This mineral gets its name from the Greek *chalkos* for copper and *anthos* for flower. When sulfate-rich waters leach copper from other minerals and then evaporate, chalcanthite will form. It is water-soluble but may be an ore mineral in areas where copper deposits are easily oxidized, particularly in arid regions. Because it precipitates

easily, chalcanthite can be found as curling (ram's horn) stalactites in copper mines and in hydrothermal vein deposits. It has a deep blue color and vitreous luster, and forms transparent to translucent crystals. Individual crystals may be prismatic or tabular, but they are usually poorly formed. It easily absorbs and loses water, and if it does so repeatedly the mineral will be reduced to a blue powder. To avoid this, fine specimens are kept in sealed, dry containers.

Chalcanthite is rare elsewhere, but it does occur in the Southwest because of the dry environment and abundance of copper. Occurrences include Yavapai and Greenlee Counties, Arizona, and Grant County, New Mexico, and commercial amounts occur in Lyon County, Nevada.

Metaphysical associations: eases feelings of life restriction or impediment
Commonly found with other copper minerals and gypsum.

CHALCOCITE
FORMULA: Cu_2S
CLASS: sulfides
CRYSTAL SYSTEM: monoclinic
HARDNESS: 2.5–3

One of the most common of all the copper minerals, chalcocite aptly gets its name from the Greek *chalkos* for "copper." It forms as a primary mineral in volcanic rocks, or as a primary or secondary mineral in ore deposits. Chalcocite is dark gray to black and opaque with dull metallic luster. When crystals are nicely formed, they will be short and prismatic with twinning forming a pseudohexagonal appearance. Massive habit is common.

Chalcocite occurs throughout the Southwest, and large crystals can be found in Cochise, Pinal, and Yavapai Counties, Arizona.

Commonly found with bornite, chalcopyrite, galena, and pyrite in primary deposits and covellite, cuprite, malachite, and azurite in secondary environments.

CHALCOPYRITE

FORMULA: $CuFeS_2$
CLASS: sulfides
CRYSTAL SYSTEM: tetragonal
HARDNESS: 3.5–4

The name comes from the Greek *chalkos* for "copper," and *pyrites* for association with "fire." Chalcopyrite is a common mineral that occurs in many geologic environments, but the most economically significant occurrences are hydrothermal ore deposits. Chalcopyrite is often confused with pyrite, because both have yellow-gold color, metallic luster, and opaque crystals. However, chalcopyrite is softer than pyrite. Chalcopyrite tarnishes to iridescent blues, greens, and yellows, and is sometimes sold as *peacock ore* (also see *bornite*, p. 27). Habit is usually massive, but crystals can be pseudotetrahedral in which each crystal face looks like a triangle with the points cut off. Twinning commonly forms striations on crystal faces.

Chalcopyrite is an important and abundant ore mineral of copper. Many other copper-ore minerals result from the alteration of chalcopyrite. It occurs as an ore mineral at many of the copper mines of Arizona. Large crystals can be found in Grant County, New Mexico.

Metaphysical associations: promotes openness to understanding other cultures
Commonly found with sphalerite, galena, pyrite, and many copper sulfides.

CHRYSOCOLLA

FORMULA: $(Cu,Al)_2H_2Si_2O_5(OH)_4 \cdot n(H_2O)$
CLASS: Silicates
CRYSTAL SYSTEM: orthorhombic
HARDNESS: 2–4

The name comes from the Greek *chrysos*, meaning "gold," and *kolla*, meaning "glue," in reference to the name of a similar-looking material used to solder gold. Chrysocolla occurs as a secondary mineral from the oxidation of copper deposits, usually as a crust on, or replacement of, earlier secondary minerals. As with many copper minerals, this one is various shades of blue, green, or turquoise. Luster can be dull, vitreous, or waxy, and specimens are translucent to opaque. In addition to crusts, this mineral's habit includes stalactitic and botryoidal masses.

While too soft to be used as a gemstone, chrysocolla can become silicified, resulting in chrysocolla-impregnated chalcedony. This material is more durable and can be polished for use as a gemstone. Chrysocolla is an ore mineral of copper. It is also commonly used as lapidary material.

Chrysocolla occurs in ore bodies throughout Arizona, including those in Gila, Greenlee, and Pinal Counties. It also occurs in Grant County, New Mexico, and Juab County, Utah.

Metaphysical associations: for ongoing inner strength and stability; maintaining patience and vitality

Commonly found with malachite.

CINNABAR
FORMULA: HgS
CLASS: sulfides
CRYSTAL SYSTEM: hexagonal
HARDNESS: 2.5

The name for this mineral comes from the Medieval Latin *cinnabaris*, traceable to the Persian *zinjifrah*, said to mean "dragon's blood." Cinnabar's appearance, with its red color and **penetration twins,** is often as dramatic as the name implies. Color can vary from bright red to purplish or brownish red with translucent to transparent crystals.

Cinnabar (red) and dolomite

Cinnabar darkens over time when it is exposed to sunlight. Luster is adamantine to submetallic. Habit is usually drusy or massive, and large, well-shaped crystals are rare.

This mineral forms in low-temperature hydrothermal deposits. Finely disseminated cinnabar in chalcedony is called *myrickite*. Cinnabar itself is soft, but myrickite is hard enough to polish and is often used in jewelry.

Cinnabar was mined by the Roman Empire for its mercury content, and it is an ore mineral of mercury even today. Mercury is poisonous, however, and miners often suffered diseases as a result. And because mercury was used when making felt products, people who made hats often suffered the mental instability caused by mercury poisoning, which is where the expression "mad as a hatter" came from.

Occurrences include Santa Clara and San Benito Counties, California; Brewster County, Texas; and Humboldt and Pershing Counties, Nevada.

Metaphysical associations: for improving cash flow and good business sense
Commonly found with pyrite, calcite, quartz, and opal.

COLEMANITE
FORMULA: $Ca_2B_6O_{11} \cdot 5(H_2O)$
CLASS: **carbonates**
CRYSTAL SYSTEM: **monoclinic**
HARDNESS: **4.5**

This mineral is named in honor of William Tell Coleman (1824–1893), a pioneer in the development of the borax industry in California. Colemanite is an ore of boron, and its abundance in California makes the state the leading producer of boron in the country. Colemanite is found as thick layers in ancient lake beds, typically in arid alkaline environments.

Crystals are often blocky or short prismatic, and colemanite can form coarse crystals or massive granular deposits. Crystals are transparent to translucent with vitreous luster. Color is gray, white, or yellow-white, with bright pale-yellow fluorescence.

Major occurrences of colemanite include Death Valley and San Bernardino and Kern Counties, California; and Clark County, Nevada.

Metaphysical associations: for getting through "dark" times
Commonly found with ulexite, gypsum, calcite, and celestine.

COPPER (NATIVE)

FORMULA: Cu
CLASS: elements
CRYSTAL SYSTEM: cubic
HARDNESS: 2.5–3

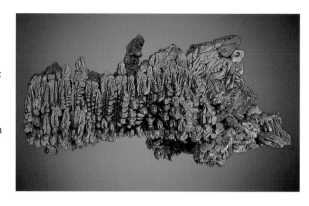

The name originates from the Greek *kyprios,* referring to Cyprus, one of the earliest places where copper was mined.

Native copper, or copper that is not chemically bound to any other element, is rare enough today that it is not economically viable as an ore mineral. Other copper minerals, such as chalcopyrite, chalcocite, malachite, azurite, and chrysocolla, are major ores of copper today. Arizona accounts for most total U.S. copper in production and value, but Utah and New Mexico are also significant producers of copper.

Crystal habit of native copper is massive or dendritic, and individual crystals are extremely rare. Copper is opaque with metallic luster and high density. Its color is copper-red.

Metaphysical associations: energizing; thought to combat arthritis and rheumatism
Commonly found with silver, calcite, zeolite, cuprite, malachite, and azurite.

COVELLITE

FORMULA: CuS
CLASS: sulfides
CRYSTAL SYSTEM: hexagonal
HARDNESS: 1.5–2

The deep midnight-blue of this mineral is what earned it the name "indigo copper." Its real name, however, comes from Nicola Covelli (1790–1829), an Italian mineralogist who discovered the mineral at Mount Vesuvius. Covellite forms as a secondary mineral, or on rare occasions as a primary mineral, in copper deposits. Very rarely does it form from volcanic gas, as it does at Mount Vesuvius. In addition to its blue color, covellite will exhibit a play of colors in yellows and reds under light. Luster is metallic to submetallic, with opaque to translucent crystals. Habit includes massive or foliated aggregates, or as coatings on other copper minerals. Nicely formed crystals are extremely rare. Occurrences include Rio Grande County, Colorado; San Juan County, Utah; and most copper mines throughout Arizona.

Metaphysical associations: for problem-solving; bringing dreams to fruition
Commonly found with bornite, chalcopyrite, and chalcocite.

CUPRITE

FORMULA: Cu_2O
CLASS: oxides
CRYSTAL SYSTEM: cubic
HARDNESS: 3.5–4

Named in 1845 from the Latin *cuprum,* meaning "copper," cuprite is commonly found as an alteration mineral resulting from the oxidation of copper-sulfide ore deposits. The color of cuprite ranges from a stunning ruby red—called "ruby copper" by miners—to reddish black. It has submetallic, adamantine, or dull luster, and crystals are translucent to semi-opaque. Crystals can form octahedra or dodecahedra. In filiform habit, cuprite can form velvet masses, in which case it is called *chalcotrichite,* or more descriptively "plush copper."

Cuprite is an ore of copper. Large, attractive ruby-red crystals occur in Cochise, Pinal, Globe, and Gila Counties, Arizona; and Grant County, New Mexico.

Metaphysical associations: energizing; release of worries
Commonly found with native copper, malachite, azurite, and chalcocite.

CYANOTRICHITE

FORMULA: $Cu_4Al_2(SO_4)(OH)_{12} \cdot 2(H_2O)$
CLASS: sulfates

CRYSTAL SYSTEM: orthorhombic
HARDNESS: 3

Hairy blue cyanotrichite

The name comes from the Greek *cyano* and *trich* for "blue" and "hair," an accurate description of this uncommon mineral that forms velvety aggregates or acicular hair-like coatings in colors ranging from sky blue to deep blue. Cyanotrichite forms as a secondary mineral in oxidized portions of copper-sulfide deposits. Crystals are translucent with silky to vitreous luster. Habit varies from acicular to drusy to rounded aggregates.

Fine specimens of cyanotrichite occur in Grand Canyon National Park and in Coconino, Cochise, Greenlee, and Yavapai Counties, Arizona; Socorro County, New Mexico; Juab County, Utah; and Pershing County, Nevada.

Metaphysical associations: courage to move forward and/or begin again
Commonly found with azurite and malachite.

DIOPTASE
FORMULA: $CuSiO_2(OH)_2$
CLASS: silicates
CRYSTAL SYSTEM: hexagonal
HARDNESS: 5

The name comes from the Greek *dia* for "through" and *optomai* for "vision," in reference to the visibility of internal cleavage planes in dioptase crystals. Dioptase forms as a secondary mineral in oxidized zones of copper deposits.

Despite its clarity and deep emerald-green color, dioptase is too soft to be used as a gemstone. However, it was thought to be emerald when it was first found. It was also thought, in the past, that looking at dioptase would improve eyesight, and wearing it around the neck would alleviate throat problems.

Dioptase has vitreous luster and translucent to transparent crystals. When nicely formed, crystals will be six-sided prismatic and usually not larger than .75 cm. Rhombohedra are also common, as are massive crusts. Dioptase can also be cryptocrystalline.

Occurrences include Pinal and Yuma Counties, Arizona, and San Bernardino County, California.

Metaphysical associations: encourages living in the moment while deeply understanding the past; heals childhood disappointments

Commonly found with chrysocolla, malachite, mimetite, wulfenite, cerussite, and quartz.

DOLOMITE
FORMULA: $CaMg(CO_3)_2$
CLASS: carbonates
CRYSTAL SYSTEM: hexagonal
HARDNESS: 3.5–4

This mineral is named in honor of Déodat de Dolomieu (1750–1801), a French geologist. Dolomite occurs as a result of **diagenesis,** or hydrothermal alteration of limestone, in high-salinity sedimentary environments, as a gangue mineral in hydrothermal ore deposits, and in carbonate sediments and marbles. Dolomite is used as a source of magnesium for industrial and medical purposes. Its color is usually light pink, but it can be colorless, white, yellow, gray, or even brown, depending on impurities. Luster is pearly, vitreous, or dull, and crystals are transparent to translucent. Its habit is commonly rhombohedral with curved faces, or it can be granular or massive. Although it looks similar to calcite, dolomite can be distinguished by its lack of effervescence in dilute hydrochloric acid unless powdered. Opaque dolomite is one of many minerals commonly used as lapidary material.

Dolomite is mined in Inyo County, California. Facet-quality colorless dolomite occurs in New Mexico.

Metaphysical associations: encourages objectivity and perspective in the face of sadness

Commonly found with various minerals, depending on the environment of formation, but including fluorite, barite, calcite, quartz, talc, serpentine, magnesite, diopside, and apatite.

EPIDOTE

FORMULA: $Ca_2(Al, Fe)_3(SiO_4)_3(OH)$
CLASS: silicates
CRYSTAL SYSTEM: monoclinic
HARDNESS: 6–7

Epidote (green) and grossular

The name comes from the Greek word *epididonai* for "increase," in reference to the mineral's typical habit of prismatic crystals with one side longer than the other. This common metamorphic mineral is found in contact zones between igneous and calcite-bearing sedimentary rocks, and forms from the alteration of feldspars, pyroxenes, and amphiboles. Its color is yellow-green, pistachio green, dark green, or black. Crystals are transparent to translucent and often are terminated by two sloping faces. In addition to the prismatic habit in which this mineral forms long, slender, striated crystals, epidote can be fibrous, granular, or massive.

Epidote has been a desirable mineral for centuries. Today, enthusiasts look for specimens for their collections, but in ancient times, epidote was sought because it was believed to help fruit and grain crops grow.

Nice specimens occur in Calaveras County, California; Chaffee County, Colorado; and Mineral County, Nevada.

Metaphysical associations: increases personal power in any aspect of life it is applied to

Commonly found with many of the common metamorphic minerals such as amphiboles, plagioclase feldspars, quartz, calcite, pyroxenes, garnet, glaucophane, and lawsonite.

FELDSPAR (GROUP)

FORMULAS: see below
CLASS: silicates
CRYSTAL SYSTEM: triclinic; sanidine and orthoclase are monoclinic
HARDNESS: 6–6.5

The name of this group comes from the German *feld,* meaning "field," and *spar,* which is a type of stone. Alkali feldspars and plagioclase feldspars make up the feldspar group. These are common rock-forming minerals and are found in igneous, metamorphic, and sedimentary rocks. Plagioclase feldspars are the most common minerals in the earth's crust. For all feldspars, habit can be blocky or tabular, with nearly rectangular or square cross-sections and slightly slanted terminations; twinning almost always occurs.

Metaphysical associations: promotes self-acceptance and release of unhealthy thought patterns

ALKALI FELDSPARS

Microcline
$KAlSi_3O_8$

The name comes from the Greek for "little" and "inclined" because when the mineral breaks, it does so at angles slightly deviating from 90 degrees. Microcline is used in the manufacture of glass, enamel, and porcelain products. Its color is usually off-white, yellowish, peach, brown, or green. Its luster is vitreous to sometimes pearly or dull if weathered. Crystals can be transparent but are usually

Microcline (blue-green) and albite (white)

translucent to opaque. A green variety of microcline often used as a semiprecious stone, called *amazonite,* occurs throughout Colorado; in Elko and Mineral Counties, Nevada; and in Inyo County, California.

Commonly found with quartz, albite, muscovite, biotite, and hornblende.

Orthoclase
$KAlSi_3O_8$

The name comes from the Greek for "straight" and "fracture," because when the mineral breaks it does so evenly along planes. Orthoclase is used in the porcelain industry. Its color is off-white, yellow, or shades of red, orange, or brown. Its luster is vitreous to dull if weathered. Crystals are usually opaque but may be translucent or, rarely, transparent. *Moonstone* is the name used for pearly and opalescent orthoclase. High-quality moonstone occurs in Catron

Twinned orthoclase

County, New Mexico. Specimens are clear and nearly colorless, with a slight tan hue and blue or silver sheen.

Commonly found with quartz, albite, muscovite, biotite, and hornblende.

Sanidine
$(K,Na)AlSi_3O_8$

This mineral's name comes from the Greek for "tablet," in reference to the mineral's tabular habit. Sanidine is used in the porcelain industry. The color is off-white, yellow, or pale shades of other colors. Its luster is

vitreous to dull if weathered, and crystals are transparent to translucent.

Commonly found with quartz, albite, muscovite, biotite, and hornblende.

PLAGIOCLASE FELDSPARS
The plagioclase feldspars form a continuous series between sodium-rich and calcium-rich end members (albite and anorthite, respectively), with the intermediate minerals

being some combination of sodium and calcium. The two end members are described here, and other plagioclase feldspars with particular qualities are included.

Albite
$NaAlSi_3O_8$

The name is derived from the Latin *albus,* meaning "white," in reference to this mineral's usual color. It is used in making ceramics. Although it's usually white, albite can be colorless or shades of blue, yellow,

Albite (white) and hematite (black)

orange, or brown. Its luster is vitreous or dull when weathered. Crystals are translucent to opaque, rarely transparent.

Commonly found with quartz, orthoclase, muscovite, biotite, and hornblende.

Anorthite
$CaAlSiO_8$

The name comes from the Greek negative prefix *an* and *orthos,* meaning straight, in reference to the mineral's oblique crystal form. It is usually white, gray, or colorless but can be pale shades of other colors. The luster is vitreous to dull if weathered, and crystals are translucent to opaque and only sometimes transparent.

Commonly found with olivine and pyroxene.

Bytownite is a calcium-rich plagioclase, usually white, gray, or colorless, that is at times used as a gem. Its luster is vitreous or dull if weathered. Crystals are translucent to opaque and rarely transparent. Gem-quality light-brown bytownite occurs in Arizona and New Mexico.

Commonly found with olivine and pyroxene.

Labradorite is an intermediate composition plagioclase. It is gray to smoky black with dull to vitreous luster and transparent to translucent crystals. What makes labradorite special is its unique blue flash of light, called "labradorescence." Gem-quality labradorite occurs in California and Nevada.

Commonly found with olivine and pyroxene.

FLUORITE

FORMULA: CaF_2
CLASS: halides
CRYSTAL SYSTEM: cubic
HARDNESS: 4

Fluorite (purple) and barite

The name fluorite comes from the Latin for "to flow," referring to the mineral's low melting point. Fluorite is easily recognized by its deep purple color, but it can also be shades of blue or green, to yellow, pink, red, black, and colorless, and it fluoresces blue under ultraviolet light. Some specimens even have different color bands. It was the variety of colors and the ease of carving that appealed to ancient Greeks and Romans, who made goblets and vases out of this mineral. Fluorite is commonly used as lapidary material.

Fluorite is found in a variety of environments, including low- to high-temperature hydrothermal deposits and as an **accessory mineral** in granites. Its luster is vitreous and crystals are translucent. The common habit is cubed, and fluorite cleaves into octahedra.

Gem-quality fluorite is produced from deposits throughout New Mexico and Utah. Excellent specimens occur throughout Arizona.

Metaphysical associations: provides psychic protection; neutralizes negative energies; improves behavior patterns; strengthens powers of concentration and perseverance

Commonly found with quartz, dolomite, calcite, barite, sulfides, topaz, scheelite, and apatite.

GALENA

FORMULA: PbS
Class: sulfides
CRYSTAL SYSTEM: cubic
HARDNESS: 2.5

Galena gets its name from the Latin *galene,* the original name used for lead ore, as it is an ore mineral of lead. Galena can also be an ore mineral of silver when silver substitutes for lead in the crystal structure. American pioneers melted galena to reduce it to native lead that was used for bullets. For the same purpose, Confederate and Union troops in the Civil War battled for control of galena deposits in eastern Missouri.

Galena is a common mineral in many sulfide deposits, and it also forms in hydrothermal vein deposits and contact metamorphic deposits. It is opaque and silver with metallic luster. Its common habit is cubed or cubes modified by octahedra. Twins, both penetration and contact, are common. This mineral can also form as fine granular aggregates.

Notable occurrences include Lake and Summit Counties, Colorado.

Metaphysical associations: harmonizing and grounding; good for invigorating investigations in the medical field

Commonly found with sphalerite, pyrite, chalcopyrite, silver minerals, siderite, calcite, dolomite, barite, and quartz.

GARNET (GROUP)

FORMULAS: see below
CLASS: silicates
CRYSTAL SYSTEM: cubic
HARDNESS: 6.5–7.5

The name "garnet" comes from the Latin words *granum* or *granites* for its resemblance to seeds of the pomegranate. Crystals form dodecahedra but can also be granular, compact, or massive. Its luster is vitreous to resinous, and crystals can be transparent to opaque.

The use of garnets as a gemstone can be traced back to prehistoric times, but their use in industry dates back only to the late 1800s, when they were first used as a coating for sandpaper. Garnet minerals all have the formula $A_3B_2(SiO_4)_3$, where A can be calcium, magnesium, ferrous iron, or manganese, and B can be aluminum, ferric iron, chromium, or, in rare instances, titanium. Garnet is well known as a gem, particularly as January's birthstone. Many deposits within the United States produce fine gem-quality garnets and three deposits are mined for industrial garnet. Presented below are a few of the better-known varieties of garnet.

Metaphysical associations: commitment and devotion; stimulates kundalini energy; stabilizes and balances energies of body, mind, and spirit; amplifies the effects of other crystals

ALMANDINE
$Fe_3Al_2Si_3O_{12}$

In White Pine County, Nevada, almandine garnet is found in deposits that accumulated by erosion of the canyon walls. The color of almandine can be deep red, brownish red, brownish black, or violet-red.

Commonly found with quartz, feldspar, micas, and tourmaline.

ANDRADITE
$Ca_3Fe_2Si_3O_{12}$

Fine-quality andradite occurs in Graham County, Arizona. Andradite can be yellow-green, green, greenish brown, orange-yellow, brown, dark gray, or black.

Commonly found with calcite in metamorphic rocks and magnetite in igneous rocks.

Andradite (brown) on diopside (white)

GROSSULAR
$Ca_3Al_2Si_3O_{12}$

High-quality, white to pale-green grossular garnet occurs in Siskiyou and Eldorado Counties, California. Other California locations for grossular are Fresno, Tulare, Butte, and Orange Counties. Large specimen-grade, apple-green grossular garnets occur in Beaver County, Utah. In general, grossular can be colorless, white, gray, yellow, yellowish green, various shades of green, brown, pink, reddish, or black.

Commonly found with quartz, calcite, and dolomite.

PYROPE
$Mg_3Al_2Si_3O_{12}$

Arizona is one of five states producing commercial amounts of garnet gems. Arizona's gem garnet, red pyrope, occurs in the northern part of Apache County on the Navajo Indian Reservation. Bright-red pyrope is also produced in San Juan County, Utah. Pyrope color ranges from purplish red to orange-red, crimson, or dark red.

Commonly found with olivine and pyroxene.

SPESSARTINE
$Mn_3Al_2Si_3O_{12}$

Fine-quality spessartine garnet comes from pegmatites in San Diego County, California. Faceting-grade spessartine garnets can be found in **vesicles** in the silicic rock on Ruby Mountain near Nathrop, Chaffee County, Colorado. Spessartine garnets also occur in several locations in White Pine County, Colorado. This variety of garnet ranges in color from red to

Spessartine (red) on albite (white)

reddish orange, orange, yellow-brown, reddish brown, or blackish brown.

Commonly found with quartz, feldspar, and micas.

GOLD (NATIVE)

FORMULA: **Au**
CLASS: **elements**
CRYSTAL SYSTEM: **cubic**
HARDNESS: **2.5–3**

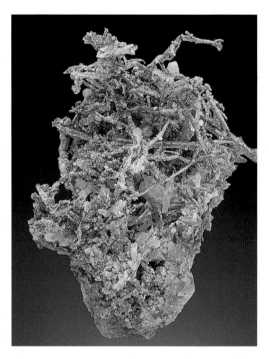

The name comes from the Old English word for the metal, possibly related to the Sanskrit *jval.* The chemical symbol comes from the Latin *aurum* meaning "shining dawn." Gold has been used for thousands of years because of its beauty as well as its resistance to chemical reaction. It is common in jewelry, and it is used in electronics because it is an excellent conductor. Gold is usually found as disseminated grains along with quartz and sulphides, or as flakes in streams and rivers, and it can also be found as veins. Mineral hunters often look for gold using metal detectors, but most deposits are under claim and require permission to access.

Nevada is the leading producer of gold in the U.S., providing more than 80 percent of the nation's supply. Colorado is third and California fifth in gold production. Gold is also produced in Utah and Arizona.

The crystal habit of native gold can be cubic, octahedral, or dodecahedral, usually rounded on the edges. Gold is also found as rounded nuggets, scales or flakes, or it can be dendritic. Gold is opaque with metallic luster and extremely high density. Its color is golden-yellow, with slight variations depending on the presence of impurities.

Metaphysical associations: spiritual purity and purification

Commonly found with pyrite, chalcopyrite, scheelite, tourmaline, and quartz.

GYPSUM

FORMULA: $Ca(SO_4) \cdot 2(H_2O)$
CLASS: **sulfates**
CRYSTAL SYSTEM: **monoclinic**
HARDNESS: **2**

The name comes from the Arabic *jibs,* meaning "plaster." It is no surprise, then, that gypsum has important industrial uses in plaster and wallboard. It is also used in cements, fertilizer, and paint. This mineral is common in sedimentary rocks, forming either by evaporation or as a

Gypsum (white) on malachite (green)

secondary mineral resulting from the hydration of anhydrite. Gypsum also forms by the reaction between sulfuric acid-bearing groundwaters and carbonate rock in an oxidizing environment, or by sulfurous volcanic gases reacting with calcium-bearing rock. Gypsum is usually white, colorless, or gray but can also be shades of red, brown, and yellow. It has vitreous to pearly luster and transparent to translucent crystals. Gypsum is usually found as massive beds resulting from precipitation out of saline waters, but it can form tabular, bladed, or blocky crystals.

Selenite is a term used to describe well-crystalline gypsum that is colorless and transparent with pearly luster. The name comes from the Greek *selini* for "moon" because of this mineral's moon-like glow. When gypsum forms long, thin crystals, it develops spirals and is called "ram's horn selenite." When gypsum forms as a fibrous aggregate, it is known as "satin spar" because it has the appearance of satin in light.

Alabaster is fine-grained massive gypsum, and it has been used for carvings for centuries. Ancient Mediterranean cultures carved statues and artifacts from alabaster, and it was common for the Etruscans to fashion sarcophagi out of alabaster. This form of gypsum is also one of many minerals commonly used as lapidary material.

Gypsum is mined throughout Colorado, Arizona, Utah, Texas, New Mexico, California, and Nevada. Large crystals occur in Wayne County, Utah; and exceptional speleothems occur in Lechuguilla Cave, Carlsbad Caverns National Park, New Mexico.

Metaphysical associations: promotes good fortune, "right thought," and improvement of character

Commonly found with calcite, aragonite, anhydrite, dolomite, and sulfur.

HEMATITE
FORMULA: Fe_2O_3
CLASS: oxides
CRYSTAL SYSTEM:
hexagonal
HARDNESS: 5.5–6.5

Hematite gets its name from the Greek *haimatites* meaning "bloodlike" because it is red when powdered. Hematite can be found in a variety of environments. It forms as an accessory mineral in silica-rich igneous rocks, as a late-stage **sublimate** in volcanic rocks, and as a deposit in hydrothermal deposits. It can also form as a product of metamorphism. It commonly results from weathering of iron-bearing minerals, particularly magnetite and pyrite. Hematite is opaque and varies in color from steel to silver-gray or black, or red to brown in earthy habit. Its luster is metallic when crystalline or dull when earthy. Its crystal habit is tabular, massive, or earthy.

A variety of hematite characterized by silvery metallic tabular crystals is called *specularite.* When hematite forms tabular crystals arranged like flower petals the specimen is called a "hematite rose."

Hematite is an ore mineral of iron, but it has been used for a variety of other purposes throughout history. The ancient Egyptians used it as a pillow for mummies. In the Middle Ages it was prescribed as a treatment for headaches and inflamed eyes, and at other times it was believed to be useful for healing wounds, snake bites, and bladder problems. Hematite is also used for pigment and is commonly used as lapidary material.

Occurrences include Juab County, Utah, and La Paz County, Arizona.

Metaphysical associations: for mental clarity, technical aptitude, confidence, and problem-solving

Commonly found with magnetite in metamorphic and igneous settings, and siderite in sedimentary environments.

JAROSITE
FORMULA: $KFe_3(SO_4)_2(OH)_6$
CLASS: sulfates

CRYSTAL SYSTEM: hexagonal
HARDNESS: 2.5–3.5

Named for the Barranco del Jaroso,
Spain, where the first analyzed
specimens were found, jarosite is a
secondary mineral that forms in
oxidized portions of sulfide-bearing
rocks, usually as an alteration of
pyrite. Although uncommon,
jarosite can also form as a low-
temperature primary hydrothermal

Jarosite (brown) and quartz (white)

mineral. Its color is amber-yellow or brown, with vitreous to resinous luster and
transparent to translucent crystals. Crystals are tabular or flattened rhombohedra, but
these are rare. Jarosite most commonly occurs as earthy masses or crusts.

Jarosite can be found throughout Arizona, particularly in Maricopa and Cochise
Counties. Other occurrences include Piute and Juab Counties, Utah, and Lincoln
County, Nevada.

Commonly found with alunite and pyrite.

LINARITE

FORMULA: $PbCu(SO_4)(OH)_2$
CLASS: sulfates
CRYSTAL SYSTEM: monoclinic
HARDNESS: 2.5

Crystals of linarite are usually quite small,
but their striking blue color makes them
hard to overlook. This uncommon
secondary mineral forms in oxidized
zones of lead-copper deposits and usually
is seen as encrustations on host rocks
with tiny protruding prismatic or tabular
crystals. Named for its occurrence in
Linares, Spain, linarite ranges from sky-
blue to deep blue with vitreous luster and
transparent to translucent crystals.

Linarite crystals can be found in Pinal and Graham Counties, Arizona; Socorro County, New Mexico; Juab County, Utah; and Inyo and San Bernardino Counties, California.

Metaphysical associations: aides contemplation, relaxation, and telepathic activity

Commonly found with anglesite, caledonite, cerussite, and malachite.

MALACHITE

FORMULA: $Cu_2(CO_3)(OH)_2$

CLASS: carbonates

CRYSTAL SYSTEM: monoclinic

HARDNESS: 3.5–4

Malachite gets its name from the Greek word *moloche,* meaning "mallows," referring to the green color of mallow leaves, and it is a common secondary mineral formed in the oxidation zone of copper deposits. Malachite is frequently banded light and dark green, a characteristic believed to be caused by variations in the crystal size; large crystals tend to be dark green and fibrous crystals tend to be lighter. Luster is dull in massive forms and silky when crystalline. Crystals are opaque in massive form and translucent when crystalline. In massive form, this mineral can be botryoidal, stalactitic, or globular. When crystals are visible, they are acicular or fibrous crusts and are almost always pseudomorphs of azurite, which means malachite replaces the chemical structure of azurite but keeps the same crystal shape.

Malachite is used as an ore of copper and is a popular stone for use in jewelry and carvings. It has had many additional uses throughout history. It was used in Europe and in the Middle East to carve charms to protect the bearer from the "evil eye." It was also given to children because it was believed to protect them from falling. Malachite carved in the form of the sun was believed to protect the bearer from venomous snakes and evil spells. The Egyptians used it for treating cholera and rheumatism. It was also known as the "sleep stone" because it was thought to charm the wearer to sleep.

Occurrences include Cochise and Greenlee Counties, Arizona; and Grant County, New Mexico.

Metaphysical associations: provides insight and clarification; assists in transforming situations for the better

Commonly found with azurite, cuprite, cerussite, chrysocolla, and calcite.

MANGANITE

FORMULA: **MnO(OH)**
CLASS: **hydroxides**
CRYSTAL SYSTEM: **monoclinic**
HARDNESS: **4**

This mineral is named for the manganese in its chemical composition and is an ore of manganese. It is an uncommon secondary mineral that forms in low-temperature hydrothermal or hot-spring manganese deposits or as a replacement of other manganese minerals in sedimentary deposits. Its color is dark gray to black with submetallic luster and opaque crystals. Its habit is commonly fibrous, granular, or massive. When crystals are visible, they are long and prismatic with flat terminations. Penetration twins are common, forming a bundle of tangled prisms.

Well-crystallized manganite is rare but occurs in Sierra County, New Mexico.

Metaphysical associations: eases "control issues" and processing of grief

Commonly found with barite, calcite, and siderite.

MICA (GROUP)

FORMULAS: **see below**
CLASS: **silicates**
CRYSTAL SYSTEM: **monoclinic**
HARDNESS: **varies**

Several minerals are included in the mica group, but the two common rock-forming minerals of this group are biotite and muscovite. Lepidolite is less common but is included for its occurrences in the Southwest.

BIOTITE

FORMULA:
$K(Fe,Mg)_3(Al,Fe)Si_3O_{10}(F,OH)_2$
HARDNESS: 2.5–3

This common rock-forming mineral is named in honor of J. B. Biot (1774–1862), a French scientist who studied micas. Strictly speaking, biotite refers to a series with end members magnesium-rich phlogopite and iron-rich annite. Since these two minerals are nearly indistinguishable without laboratory analysis, the term biotite is used for black micas and *phlogopite* for brown. Biotite is found in many environments and is particularly abundant in igneous and metamorphic rocks. Luster is submetallic, vitreous, or pearly, and crystals are semi-transparent. When weathered, biotite will appear golden and sparkly. Foliated "books" of biotite can occur, but this mineral is usually found as disseminated flakes. Biotite has important industrial applications as a heat insulator.

Biotite, along with other micas, is mined in Yavapai County, Arizona, and Taos County, New Mexico.

Metaphysical associations: ability to see clearly and objectively

Commonly found with quartz, potassium feldspar, plagioclase feldspar, muscovite, pyroxenes, and garnet.

LEPIDOLITE

FORMULA: $K(Li,Al)_3Al(Al, Si)_4O_{10}(F,OH)_2$
HARDNESS: 2.5–4

Lepidolite gets its name from the Greek *lepid* meaning "flake" or "scale," because of the mineral's common habit as coarse- to fine-grained scaly aggregates. This mineral occurs in granite pegmatites by alteration of muscovite or biotite, as well as in high-temperature quartz veins and **greisens.** The color is usually violet to red but can be gray or yellow. Lepidolite has a vitreous luster with transparent to translucent crystals.

Lepidolite is commonly used as lapidary material and is an ore of lithium. Occurrences include San Diego County, California, and Gunnison County, Colorado.

Metaphysical associations: encourages one to let go of unproductive emotional patterns

Commonly found with elbaite, cassiterite, topaz, beryl, tourmaline, and micas.

MUSCOVITE

Formula:
$$KAl_2(Si_3Al)O_{10}(OH,F)_2$$
Hardness: 2–2.5

The name comes from its occurrence in Moscow, Russia, where it was used in the making of windowpanes. Muscovite is a common rock-forming mineral in metamorphic and igneous rocks, and it can form from other minerals as a result of hydrothermal alteration. Its color is usually silver but can be white, yellow, green, or brown. Crystals are transparent to translucent. Muscovite usually forms books of platy aggregates that easily separate into thin sheets along cleavage planes. Individual crystals are tabular to columnar.

Muscovite is used as an insulator in electrical equipment. It is mined in Yavapai County, Arizona, and Taos County, New Mexico.

Metaphysical associations: mystical awareness of higher planes; overcoming self-doubt

Commonly found with quartz, plagioclase feldspar, alkali feldspar, biotite, tourmaline, and topaz.

MIMETITE

FORMULA: $Pb_5(AsO_4)_3Cl$
CLASS: phosphates
CRYSTAL SYSTEM: hexagonal
HARDNESS: 3.5–4

This mineral gets its name from the Greek *mimetes,* which means "imitator," in reference to its resemblance to the mineral pyromorphite. The color is yellow to deep orange but can be brown, green, gray, or colorless. Its luster is resinous to adamantine and crystals are transparent to translucent. Mimetite can form as six-sided barrel-shaped prisms, but it is commonly found as botryoidal crusts, sparkling aggregates, small spherical masses, or spike-like crystals.

Occurrences include Pinal and Maricopa Counties, Arizona, and Juab County, Utah.
Metaphysical associations: encourages an attitude of enthusiasm for life
Commonly found with wulfenite, calcite, barite, and galena.

MOLYBDENITE

FORMULA: MoS_2
CLASS: sulfides
CRYSTAL SYSTEM: hexagonal
HARDNESS: 1–1.5

Molybdenite gets its name from the Greek *molybdos,* meaning "lead." While this mineral does not contain lead, the name is believed to be the result of misidentification by early mineralogists. This mineral can be found in a variety of geological environments, including copper deposits and hydrothermal vein deposits. Its color is silver or lead-gray with metallic luster and

Molybdenite (gray metallic) on quartz (white)

opaque crystals. Its habit is typically plates or stubby prisms, but molybdenite bends easily so specimens may be misshapen. This mineral looks rather like graphite and has a similar greasy feel, but it is heavier and more silver. Molybdenite is a major source of molybdenum and occurs throughout the Southwest.

Commonly found with scheelite, cassiterite, and pyrite.

MOTTRAMITE

FORMULA: $PbCu(VO_4)(OH)$
CLASS: vandates
CRYSTAL SYSTEM: orthorhombic
HARDNESS: 3–3.5

Mottramite is named for an occurrence in England at Mottram St. Andrew, Cheshire. It usually forms as a secondary mineral in the oxidized zone of vanadium-bearing base metal deposits. Mottramite is typically various shades of dark green but can also be black. It has a resinous

luster and its crystals are transparent to opaque. Its habits are drusy, radiating or stalactitic masses. This mineral is the copper-rich end member of the descloizite series. Descloizite is the zinc-rich end member and the more common of the two minerals.

Occurrences include Pinal, Cochise, and Gila Counties, Arizona; Socorro County, New Mexico; and Clark County, Nevada.

Metaphysical associations: learning from present situations in order to set appropriate goals
Commonly found with mimetite, wulfenite, cerussite, azurite, and dioptase.

OLIVINE (GROUP)

FORMULA: $(Mg,Fe)_2SiO_4$
CLASS: silicates
CRYSTAL SYSTEM:
orthorhombic
HARDNESS: 6.5

Peridot (see Forsterite, below)

Olivine is a continuous mineral series with two end members—iron-rich fayalite and magnesium-rich forsterite. The term "olivine" is used to refer to minerals of intermediate composition between the two end members, and when speaking in general terms it can refer to the end member minerals as well. Olivine is an important mineral as a gem (peridot), for its industrial use in abrasives, and as an ore of magnesium. Olivine is typically found as grains that have weathered out of other material or as granular pieces of rock in basaltic rock. Massive habit is common. Its color is a light near-emerald green to the more common pale yellowish green; it's also found colorless, and greenish brown to black. Its luster is vitreous, and crystals are transparent to translucent.

Metaphysical associations: letting go of counterproductive associations, relationships, and ideas (as forsterite or peridot)

FAYALITE

This mineral gets its name from Faial (Fayal) Island in the Azores, where it was thought to occur in volcanic rock. It was later found to have been transported in slag carried as ballast for ships.

Commonly found with pyroxenes, plagioclase feldspars, and amphiboles.

FORSTERITE

This mineral is named in honor of Adolarius Jacob Forster (1739–1806), an English mineral collector and dealer. Forsterite is probably best known as *peridot,* a popular gem and August's birthstone. Peridot gets its light-green color from traces of iron in the crystal structure. In comparison, fayalite's high iron content results in dark-green minerals that are less desirable for use as gems.

Peridot Mesa, located on the San Carlos Apache Indian Reservation in Gila County, Arizona, is the most productive locality in the world for peridot; perhaps 80 to 95 percent of the world's peridot comes from there. The peridot occurs in xenoliths—pieces of pre-existing rock—that were brought up from the mantle as a result of basaltic volcanism. Peridot is also produced from a deposit in Apache County, Arizona. Gem-quality peridot occurs in McKinley County, New Mexico, as well as in the southeastern part of that state.

Commonly found with pyroxenes, plagioclase feldspars, and amphiboles.

OPAL

FORMULA: $SiO_2 \cdot n(H_2O)$
CLASS: **mineraloids**
CRYSTAL SYSTEM: **amorphous**
HARDNESS: **5.5–6**

The name "opal" is derived from the Sanskrit *upala,* the word for "precious stone." For many centuries it has been considered a valuable stone for its beauty and power. The early Greeks believed an opal would bestow on its owner the power of prophecy and foresight. To the Romans it was a symbol of hope and purity. While it is still popular as October's birthstone, an opal is not technically a mineral by the strictest definition because it does not have a long-range ordered crystal structure.

Opal is formed of tiny spheres of silica gel arranged in close-packed arrays. Interaction of light with these arrays results in a play of colors that varies depending on the size and consistency of the spherules.

Opal occurs as cavity-fillings in fractures and geodes, as nodules, or as a replacement of other minerals and wood. Opal is white, colorless, pale yellow, pale red, light blue, brown, gray, or black. Common opal lacks color and luster, whereas precious opal has vitreous to pearly luster. Specimens are transparent to opaque. Common opal is often used as lapidary material for carvings; precious opal is used for jewelry.

Virgin Valley, Nevada, is known for its precious opal. This source was first discovered in the early 1900s. Opal from this area is comparable to the world's best in terms of its size and play of color. The material varies in body color from deep black to brown, yellowish-white, white, or colorless. The play of color is red, blue, green, yellow, and orange. The opal occurs mainly as replacements of wood or conifer cones, but some can be found as nodules filling voids in clay deposits. Opal from Virgin Valley has limited use because of its tendency to develop fine cracks along its surface, a process called "crazing." Because of this the opal is not well suited for use in jewelry, but it can be a beautiful addition to mineral collections when displayed in water, glycerine, mineral oil, or another liquid.

Precious opal also occurs in Humboldt and Nye Counties, Nevada, although the play of color is not as good as that of opal from Virgin Valley, and it has the same problem with crazing. Arizona produces precious opal that is light blue with a play of red, blue, green, and orange. These precious-opal locations and many other locations around the Southwest also produce common opal and opalized wood.

Metaphysical associations: enhances one's true character and potential
Commonly found with quartz and other silica-rich volcanic rocks.

PETRIFIED WOOD

FORMULA, CLASS, CRYSTAL SYSTEM, AND HARDNESS:
see description that follows

The southwestern United States is known for its petrified wood, particularly from the Petrified Forest National Park in Arizona, which is said to contain the most colorful silicified logs in the world.

Petrified wood is not a mineral itself, and therefore does not have a formula, class, crystal system, or hardness of its own. It forms when a tree's organic cells are replaced by a mineral. The petrified wood found in the southwestern U.S. formed 225 million years ago, when what was once a forest became buried by water and sediment and stayed buried for millions of years. The sediment contained volcanic ash, which is high in silica. The silica and other elements dissolved in the water, seeped into the wood cells, and crystallized into chalcedony. Trace elements traveling with the silica determine the color of the petrified wood. For example, manganese causes the chalcedony in the wood to be pink; iron causes red, brown, and yellow colors; and copper causes green and blue.

Native Americans of Jemez Pueblo in New Mexico adorn pieces of petrified wood with feathers and beads for use in rituals.

Petrified wood ranks high in value of commercially produced gemstones in Arizona. In addition to Arizona, petrified wood can be found in Utah, in various locations around the Escalante River and in the Coyote Buttes region near the Paria River; and in the Bisti Badlands in New Mexico.

Metaphysical associations: grounding, support, and strength in all areas of life

PYRITE

FORMULA: FeS_2
CLASS: sulfides
CRYSTAL SYSTEM: cubic
HARDNESS: 6–6.5

The name for this mineral comes from the Greek word *pyr,* meaning "fire," because it will spark when struck by steel. Pyrite is also known as "fool's gold" because of its gold color and metallic luster. This mineral is commonly found in all sulfide ore deposits. It forms as an accessory mineral in igneous rocks  and contact metamorphic deposits, and as diagenetic replacements in sedimentary rocks. Pyrite also replaces organic material in coal, wood, or shells. It is brassy yellow with metallic luster and opaque crystals. Pyrite typically forms cubes, octahedra or pyritohedra (a 12-faced form with each face shaped as a pentagon). Striations are often seen on crystal faces, and penetration twins are common. When pyritohedra form penetration twins, they are called "iron crosses." Flattened reniform nodules called "pyrite dollars" are popular in rock shops. Pyrite was used as a source of sulfur in the past.

Large crystals occur in Santa Cruz County, Arizona, and Lake County, Colorado.

Metaphysical associations: protection from negativity; seeing through false fronts

Commonly found with galena, sphalerite, chalcopyrite, hematite, fluorite, quartz, barite, and calcite.

PYROLUSITE

FORMULA: MnO_2

CLASS: **oxides**

CRYSTAL SYSTEM: **tetragonal**

HARDNESS: **6–6.5**

The name comes from the Greek *pyr* and *louein,* meaning "fire" and "to wash," referring to its use in removing tints in the manufacturing of glass. This secondary mineral forms from hydrothermal alteration of massive manganese-bearing deposits and in hydrothermal vein deposits. It also forms in bogs and lakes and in shallow marine environments. Its color is steel-gray to a solid black, and its luster is metallic to dull in weathered specimens or thin crusts. Crystals are opaque but can be translucent when very thin. Rarely, crystals form perfect prisms, but pyrolusite more commonly forms as a replacement of manganite. This mineral may also be fibrous or reniform and can form as a crust or as dendrites on sandstones and siltstone, often resembling plant fossils. Pyrolusite is an ore of manganese.

Occurrences include Lake County, Colorado; Sierra County, New Mexico; and Mohave County, Arizona.

Metaphysical associations: beneficial for "starting over" in major life changes; for staying true to oneself

Commonly found with manganite and hematite.

PYROPHYLLITE

FORMULA: $Al_2Si_4O_{10}(OH)_2$
CLASS: silicates
CRYSTAL SYSTEM: triclinic
HARDNESS: 1–2

This mineral's name comes from the Greek *pyr* and *phyllon,* meaning "fire" and "leaf," referring to the flaking of the mineral upon heating, which is a result of the water molecules being driven off. This mineral forms from hydrothermal alteration as well as in metamorphic rocks. The color ranges from white to gray, yellow, pale green, or blue, and even colorless. Luster is greasy to dull with pearly surfaces. Crystals are translucent to opaque. Individual crystals are rare, as pyrophyllite commonly forms fibrous and lamellar masses.

Pyrophyllite is used in ceramics and as a filler for rubber products and paints.

Occurrences include Imperial, Mariposa, and Mono Counties, California; and La Paz County, Arizona.

Commonly found with topaz, mica, and quartz.

QUARTZ

FORMULA: (SiO_2)
CLASS: silicates
CRYSTAL SYSTEM: hexagonal
HARDNESS: 7

Note: Quartz is not a mineral "group." All minerals in this category are, strictly speaking, quartz because they all have the same chemical formula and crystal system. Trace elements, inclusions, crystal size, and so on, can dramatically change the way a mineral looks, and this is often the case with quartz. Many types of quartz, therefore, have been given their own descriptive names, as listed here.

Scepter quartz: growth inhibition forms the narrow stem, and new growth results in the crown

Quartz is found in all types of rocks and geological environments, and it is a major component of granites, sandstones, quartzites, carbonate rocks, and hydrothermal vein deposits. It is used in the production of glass, electrical components, optical lenses, and abrasives. It is also used as a gem. The most common habit is prismatic terminated with a six-

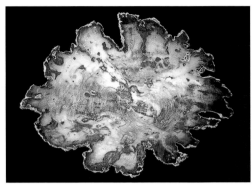

Agatized petrified wood

sided pyramid. In some cases, three of the six sides may dominate and cause the pyramid to look three-sided. Drusy forms are common, and massive forms include botryoidal, globular, and stalactitic crusts. While pure quartz is colorless to white, trace elements can color it rose, yellow, green, blue, violet, brown, or black. Its luster is vitreous, and crystals are transparent to nearly opaque. The name comes from the German *Quarz,* but quartz is known by many different names depending on its color and form. Here are a few of the most common ones:

AMETHYST

Amethyst is well known as February's birthstone and is easily recognizable by its purple color and prismatic, translucent, vitreous crystals. The color is the result of very minor amounts of iron impurities in the crystal structure. The name comes from the Greek word

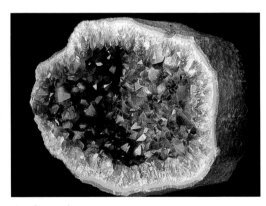

Amethyst geode

amethustos, meaning "not drunken"; the ancient Egyptians believed that wearing amethyst would keep one from becoming intoxicated when drinking alcoholic beverages.

Metaphysical associations: balances energies of body, mind, emotions; good for meditation, easing tension; gives serenity

CHALCEDONY

Chalcedony is generally used as an umbrella term encompassing the many microcrystalline quartz stones. Chalcedony occurs in many colors and in a variety of environments, but two of the best-known varieties of chalcedony are *jasper* and *agate*. *Jasper* is a dense, opaque variety of chalcedony colored by iron oxides forming red, brown, or yellow specimens. *Agate,* a term used to describe a banded form of chalcedony, can be broken down into further classifications, including the following:

Fire agate

This form of chalcedony contains inclusions of iron oxides that cause a play of colors much like that of precious opal. Arizona is the only state currently to produce fire agate with commercial operations or dig-for-fee production. The material is produced in Graham, Greenlee, Maricopa, Mohave, and Yuma Counties.

Mohave Blue Agate

This pastel blue to blue-gray material is commercially produced from deposits in California. It is a popular mineral for jewelry and carvings.

Onyx

This term refers to agate that is banded black and white. In the Middle Ages, onyx was used to ward off the "evil eye." *Sardonyx* is similar, but refers to brown-banded varieties.

Colorado, Utah, and Texas have deposits of high-quality jasper and agate throughout the state.

Metaphysical associations: promotes goodwill and reduces hostility; telepathy; eases self-doubt; assists with problem-solving; heals old sorrows (onyx)

GEODES

Geodes are popular specimens for many rock collectors. Their rounded, modest-looking exteriors disguise hollow interiors lined with beautifully formed amethyst crystals or filled with agate or jasper.

The name comes from the Greek *geoides,* meaning "earthlike," in reference to the rock's spherical shape. Geodes form in sedimentary and volcanic rocks when rounded cavities are filled with minerals precipitated from slowly moving groundwater. While geodes are not a *type* of quartz, they are most often *filled* with massive or crystalline quartz. If the minerals are deposited quickly, the result will be chalcedony, but if the deposit happens over a longer period of time, quartz crystals will have a chance to form. The outer mineral layer, usually of chalcedony or limestone, is resistant to weathering, which is why the geode remains as a spherical body after the rock around it has weathered away.

Other common minerals in geodes include those that are highly soluble in water, such as calcite or halite.

Smoky quartz

ROCK CRYSTAL QUARTZ

The clear variety of quartz that is most commonly used for gems is called rock crystal quartz. Several deposits in California produce significant amounts of quality rock crystal. Cobbles and round crystals have been found in streambeds in Amador and Calaveras Counties (in California). Fine rock crystal also occurs in pegmatites in San Diego County. Arizona, Colorado, and Nevada each produce some rock crystal.

Metaphysical associations: unconditional love; calming; reinstates love of the self

ROSE QUARTZ

Light pink in color, rose quartz is usually found as a massive deposit. The color results from fibrous nanoinclusions of another mineral such as dumortierite.

Metaphysical associations: balances energies of body, mind, emotions; good for meditation, easing tension, emotional healing; gives serenity

OTHER QUARTZ VARIETIES include *milky quartz,* in which fluid inclusions in the mineral cause a cloudy white appearance; *smoky quartz,* the gray-brown to black variety resulting from exposure to naturally occurring radioactive elements; and *citrine,* a yellow to orange gemstone variety resulting from small amounts of iron. Citrine is rare in nature but can be created by heating amethyst.

All quartz varieties are commonly found with basic rock-forming minerals such as calcite, feldspar, and mica.

RHODOCHROSITE

Formula: $Mn(CO_3)$
Class: carbonates
Crystal system: hexagonal
Hardness: 3.5–4

Rhodochrosite (red) with quartz (white) and tetrahedrite (gray)

This mineral gets its name from the Greek *rhod* and *chrÿs,* meaning "rose" and "color," in reference to the mineral's typical color. Rhodochrosite forms as a primary mineral in low- to moderate-temperature hydrothermal ore bodies and as a secondary mineral in sediments and metamorphic deposits. It is easily identified because of its distinct color and beauty. In spite of the name, this mineral does not occur only as red or pink specimens, but can be white, yellow, or brown. Its luster is vitreous or pearly with transparent to translucent crystals. Rhodochrosite in stalactitic form can be sliced to show concentric white and pink banding. Rhodochrosite is usually massive, but it can occur as granular, columnar, or crusty. Rare individual crystals form rhombohedra.

Rhodochrosite is an ore of manganese. It is commonly used as a lapidary material by Native Americans in the Southwest; most of the rhodochrosite used for this purpose, however, comes from Argentina.

Rhodochrosite is the state mineral of Colorado because fine-quality, bright red, well-formed, facet-grade crystals can be found in parts of the state, particularly in Park County. Other occurrences include Santa Cruz County, Arizona; and Lake, San Juan, and Ouray Counties, Colorado.

Metaphysical associations: renewal of body and relationships; stone for healing the earth; promotes positive attitude

Commonly found with calcite, siderite, dolomite, fluorite, barite, quartz, pyrite, sphalerite, and garnet.

ROSASITE

FORMULA: $(Cu,Zn)_2(CO_3)(OH)_2$
CLASS: carbonates
CRYSTAL SYSTEM: monoclinic
HARDNESS: 4.5

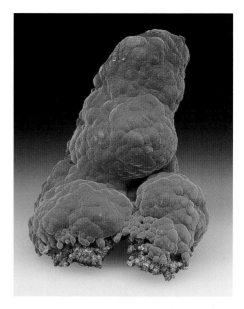

Rosasite, named for its occurrence in the Rosas mine in Sardinia, Italy, is an uncommon secondary mineral formed in the oxidized zone of ore deposits containing copper and zinc minerals. Its color is usually a bluish-green to green with silky to vitreous luster, or dull for massive forms. Crystals are transparent to translucent. Rosasite can form as radiating acicular crystals, botryoidal crusts, or nodules.

Occurrences include Socorro County, New Mexico; Cochise and Gila Counties, Arizona; San Bernardino County, California; Lake County, Colorado; Pershing County, Nevada; and Tooele County, Utah.

Metaphysical associations: calms the emotions; helps one gain personal insight
Commonly found with malachite, aurichalcite, smithsonite, and cerussite.

SCHEELITE

FORMULA: $Ca(WO_4)$
CLASS: tungstates
CRYSTAL SYSTEM: tetragonal
HARDNESS: 4.5–5

Named for the discoverer of tungsten, Karl Wilhelm Scheele, scheelite is a high-temperature mineral found in hydrothermal vein deposits and greisen, and less commonly in granite pegmatites. Its color is white, yellow, orange, or greenish gray to brown. Luster is adamantine to greasy, and crystals are transparent to translucent. This mineral commonly forms massive, columnar, or granular aggregates. Scheelite has strong blue-white fluorescence, and prospectors search for it at night using ultraviolet lights.

Most of the world's tungsten supply comes from the mineral wolframite, but because scheelite is especially abundant in the U.S., this mineral provides the United States with most of its tungsten.

In California, large fine-quality brown to yellow stones occur in Mohave County, and large colorless stones occur in Kern and Inyo Counties. Utah produces facet-grade scheelite, and large crystals are found in Cochise County, Arizona. Scheelite is commercially mined in Inyo County, California.

Scheelite (brownish orange) and quartz

Metaphysical associations: facilitates focused, connected thought patterns

Minerals that scheelite is commonly found with vary, depending on the environment in which it forms, but they include cassiterite, topaz, fluorite, apatite, tourmaline, quartz, grossular, and vesuvianite.

SERPENTINE (GROUP)
FORMULA: $(Mg,Fe)_6Si_4O_{10}(OH)_8$
CLASS: silicates
CRYSTAL SYSTEM: monoclinic
HARDNESS: see below

Serpentine is a group of minerals with similar chemistry but slightly different structures. In general, serpentines are major rock-forming minerals found in metamorphic and weathered igneous rocks. Color is olive green, yellow or golden, brown, or black. Luster is greasy, waxy or silky. Crystals are translucent and masses are opaque. Veins of fibrous serpentine can be found inside massive serpentines.

Serpentine is one of several minerals commonly used as a lapidary material. It's common and widespread. Clinochrysotile is confirmed to occur in Gila County, Arizona. Two of the best-known minerals in this group are antigorite and chrysotile.

Metaphysical associations: finding the best course of action; advancement; resourcefulness and integrity

Commonly found with olivine, garnet, biotite, and talc.

ANTIGORITE

This mineral is named for its occurrence at Val Antigorio, Italy. Typical habit is fine-grained massive or platy aggregates. Antigorite is green and has a hardness of 3–4.

CHRYSOTILE

The name for this mineral comes from the Greek *chrysos* for "golden" and *tilos* for "fibers." This mineral is used in brake linings and fireproof fabrics. Its common habit is fibrous asbestiform. Chrysotile is actually a generic term for asbestiform serpentine and can be classified further as *clinochrysotile, orthochrysotile,* or *parachrysotile* depending on the mineral's structure. While nonfibrous serpentine is not a cancer concern, asbestos serpentines should be kept in closed containers. Chrysotile has a hardness of 3–5.

SIDERITE

FORMULA: $Fe(CO_3)$
CLASS: carbonates
CRYSTAL SYSTEM: hexagonal
HARDNESS: 3.5–4

The name comes from the Greek *sideros,* meaning "iron." Siderite is a common mineral found in hydrothermal vein deposits, as a rock-forming mineral in limestone or clay, as a replacement mineral in limestone, and less commonly in metamorphic rocks. Its color is gray, yellow,

yellowish brown, greenish brown, reddish brown, or brown. The surface may appear iridescent from weathering. Crystals are translucent with vitreous luster. Crystals form rhombohedra, often with curved faces. Siderite can also be found in globular, botryoidal, stalactitic, vein-filling, and earthy aggregates.

Occurrences include Cochise and Mohave Counties, Arizona; and Lake County, Colorado.

Metaphysical associations: renews focus on one's life "calling"; facilitates alignment of the body's chakras and meridians

Commonly found with quartz, barite, fluorite, galena, chalcopyrite, and pyrite.

SILVER (NATIVE)

Formula: Ag
Class: elements
Crystal system: cubic
Hardness: 2.5–3

The name originates from the Old English *soelfer,* related to the German *silber* and the Dutch *zilver.* Silver forms primarily as a hydrothermal mineral. It is commonly used in jewelry, utensils, and coins, and has applications in photographic processing.

The crystal habit of native silver is commonly elongated or wiry, or found as massive sheets and coatings. Silver is opaque with metallic luster and high density. Its color, naturally, is silver, but the surface tarnishes easily to gray or black.

Nevada ranks second in the country for silver production, accounting for nearly 24 percent of the silver produced from U.S. mines. Utah is fourth in the production of silver. Silver is also produced in Arizona, Colorado, and California.

Metaphysical associations: provides insight into the self; patience and perseverance; ability to move forward without being judgmental

Commonly found with gold and copper.

SMITHSONITE

FORMULA: $Zn(CO_3)$
CLASS: **carbonates**
CRYSTAL SYSTEM: **hexagonal**
HARDNESS: **4–4.5**

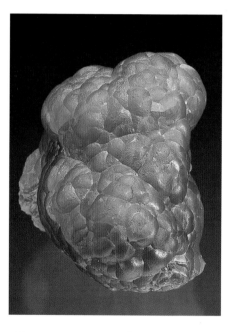

Smithsonite is named for James Smithson (1765–1829), the founder of the Smithsonian Institution. Its color is often apple green, but it depends on the impurities in the mineral. Copper will give a blue-green color, manganese or cobalt a violet color, and iron a brown color. Cadmium impurities result in yellow smithsonite known as "turkey-fat ore." Regardless of crystal color, the streak—or powder—of this mineral is always white. Smithsonite has an unusually striking vitreous to pearly luster with transparent to translucent crystals. Its habit can be curved rhombohedrons or scalenohedrons but is typically botryoidal or globular.

It's found as a secondary mineral in zinc deposits and was used as a source of zinc in the past.

Fine samples occur in Socorro County, New Mexico. Smithsonite also occurs as an ore in Lake County, Colorado, and Pinal County, Arizona.

Metaphysical associations: may increase clairvoyance; offers comfort and gentleness for navigating difficulties; heals effects of emotional abuse

Commonly found with sphalerite, cerussite, malachite, and azurite.

SPHALERITE

FORMULA: ZnS
CLASS: sulfides
CRYSTAL SYSTEM: cubic
HARDNESS: 3.5–4

Sphalerite (black) and amethyst

From the Greek *sphaleros,* the name of this mineral means "treacherous," because of what was thought to be a lack of metal in this metallic mineral. When sphalerite was smelted, no metal was produced—or so it was thought. It was later discovered that the material coating the furnace walls could be resmelted with copper to form brass. These coatings were zinc oxide that formed from zinc vapors, because, it was discovered, zinc vaporizes at normal smelting temperatures.

Sphalerite is a common mineral that can be found in hydrothermal ore deposits, in association with iron sulfides or in carbonate-rich environments. It can be yellow, brown, red, green, or black with transparent to opaque crystals and submetallic to metallic luster. Crystals can form combinations of tetrahedra, dodecahedra, and cubes, but sphalerite most commonly forms as masses. Sphalerite is an ore of zinc.

Deposits in Colorado, including Eagle County, and in Utah produce facet-grade sphalerite.

Metaphysical associations: assists one in knowing the truth—be it one's life purpose, seeing through deceit, or accessing psychic information

Commonly found with galena, chalcopyrite, pyrite, barite, fluorite, carbonates, and quartz.

TALC

FORMULA: $Mg_3Si_4O_{10}(OH)_2$
CLASS: silicates
CRYSTAL SYSTEM: monoclinic
HARDNESS: 1

Most people are familiar with talc as the main ingredient in talcum powder and an additive in many cosmetics, but its resistance to heat, electricity, and acids make it useful in many other ways, including as a material in countertops and electrical switchboards. It is also used as an ingredient in paints, rubber, roofing materials, ceramics, and insecticides.

The origin of this mineral's name is uncertain, but it possibly comes from the Arabic *talq,* meaning "pure," in reference to the color of its powder. Talc is a primary mineral in metamorphic rocks such as marbles, and less commonly a secondary mineral in magnesium-rich igneous rocks.

The massive form, called *soapstone,* has been used for thousands of years as a material for carving. Early cultures made cooking vessels out of soapstone.

Talc forms foliated masses and is soft enough to be scratched by a fingernail. Its color is white, green, gray, or brown. Luster is dull to pearly or greasy, and masses are opaque with a soapy feel.

Talc is mined in San Bernardino County, California; and Hudspeth and Culberson Counties, Texas.

Commonly found with chlorite, serpentine, dolomite, and calcite.

TENNANTITE

FORMULA: $(Cu,Ag,Zn,Fe)_{12}As_4S_{13}$
CLASS: sulfides
CRYSTAL SYSTEM: cubic
HARDNESS: 3–4.5

Named after Smithson Tennant (1761–1815), an English chemist, tennantite occurs in hydrothermal vein deposits and contact metamorphic deposits. Its color is black to steel-gray with a metallic luster and opaque crystals. This mineral can form

Tennantite (black) and quartz

tetrahedral crystals or can occur in massive or granular form. Tennantite is a source of arsenic.

This mineral occurs in many localities in Colorado including Clear Creek, Gilpin, Pitkin, and San Juan Counties.

Metaphysical associations: helps safely uncover buried emotions and lost dreams
Commonly found with pyrite, calcite, dolomite, siderite, barite, fluorite, and quartz.

TOURMALINE (GROUP)

FORMULAS: **see below**
CLASS: **silicates**
CRYSTAL SYSTEM: **hexagonal**
HARDNESS: **7**

The name comes from the Sinhalese *toramalli,* which is the name given to what was thought to be colored zircons on the island of Sri Lanka (Ceylon). These "zircons" were later found to be tourmaline.

The tourmaline group has a general formula of $AX_3Y_6(BO_3)_3Si_6O_{18}(O,OH,F)_4$. The A can be either calcium or sodium. The X can be aluminum, iron, lithium, or magnesium. The Y is usually aluminum but can also be chromium or iron.

Its crystal habit is typically elongated three-sided prisms, appearing predomionantly triangular in cross section. The terminations can be pyramidal or flat. The prism faces have lengthwise striations. Acicular and massive forms can occur.

Tourmalines can be colorless or can exhibit virtually any color. Even an individual crystal can vary in color along its length or in cross section. Those that vary in color along their length form bicolor and tricolor specimens, and color combinations are many and varied. Those that vary in cross section from center to edge form attractive specimens such as "watermelon" tourmaline—a crystal with a pink core and green "rind."

The wealth and quality of tourmalines in California were first discovered

Elbaite, from the tourmaline group

by the gemstone industry in the late 1800s. Since then, California, particularly Riverside and San Diego Counties, has produced more tourmaline in quantity and value than probably any other area except Brazil. There are many mineral members in the tourmaline group. Two of the most common are elbaite and schorl.

Metaphysical associations: purifies spiritual energy; used as a shamanic protector; aids in psychological insight; helps balance the two hemispheres of the brain

Commonly found with micas, feldspars, and quartz.

ELBAITE
$Na(Al, Li)_3Al_6B_3O_9Si_6O_{18}(OH)_4$

Elbaite is often used as a gemstone. It varies in color from red to pink, green, blue, orange, or yellow. Its luster is vitreous and crystals are transparent to translucent.

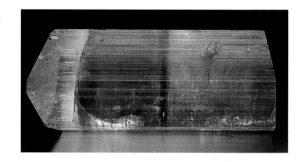

SCHORL
$NaFe_3Al_6B_3O_9Si_6O_{18}(OH)_4$

Schorl, an iron-rich tourmaline, is the most abundant of the tourmalines and is a common accessory mineral, and sometimes a major component, in igneous and metamorphic rocks. Schorl is black with a vitreous to submetallic luster and opaque crystals. Long, thin crystals of schorl are common as inclusions in quartz. Such specimens are called "tourmalinated quartz." These specimens display long schorl needles crisscrossing in colorless quartz.

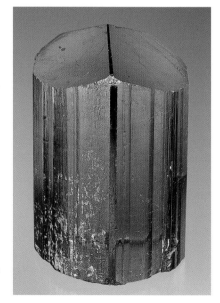

TURQUOISE

FORMULA: $CuAl_6(PO_4)_4(OH)_8 \cdot 4(H_2O)$
CLASS: phosphates
CRYSTAL SYSTEM: triclinic
HARDNESS: 5–6

The name of this mineral comes from the Anglo-French *turkeise,* meaning "Turkish," in reference to the source of the original stones imported into Europe. Turquoise is formed when groundwater interacts with aluminum-rich rock in the presence of copper. It's no surprise, then, that Arizona's many copper deposits result in the production of some of the world's finest turquoise specimens.

Turquoise has been mined for thousands of years. The early Egyptians mined it at least as early as 6000 B.C., and the indigenous peoples of the southwestern U.S. and Mexico have mined and used it extensively since 200 B.C. In the late 1800s, the mineral industry discovered high-quality deposits in the Southwest. Before that, the world's best turquoise was found in Persia (now Iran).

The United States is the world's largest producer of turquoise, with the southwestern states generating most of the supply. Arizona ranks highest among the states in terms of value and production of turquoise, as much of this mineral is mined as a byproduct from copper mines. Nevada is also a major producer of turquoise, and the material there generally occurs in various shades of blues and greens. Some turquoise from Nevada contains iron, making it pale-green to yellow.

Its habit is usually cryptocrystalline nodules and small veins. Crystals large enough to be seen are very rare. The trademark of this mineral is its well-known color, but turquoise actually can vary from greenish blue to sky-blue shades. Luster is dull to waxy, and cryptocrystalline forms are opaque.

Turquoise is commonly used as lapidary material, particularly by Native Americans in the Southwest. Most turquoise on the market is treated to make it more durable and easier to carve.

In Arizona, commercial deposits occur in many areas including Mohave, Greenlee, and Gila Counties. In California, turquoise deposits are found in San Bernardino, Imperial, and Inyo Counties. Numerous small deposits occur throughout Nevada.

Metaphysical associations: to maintain grounding during deep meditation; promotes safe, loving communication of emotional truths; purification; protection of property; a friendship stone

Commonly found with variscite and chalcedony.

ULEXITE

FORMULA: $NaCaB_5O_6(OH)_6 \cdot 5(H_2O)$
CLASS: carbonates
CRYSTAL SYSTEM: triclinic
HARDNESS: 2.5

Named in honor of George Ludwig Ulex (1811–1883), a German chemist who provided the first reliable analysis of the material, ulexite is an ore of boron. It is also a popular mineral in rock shops, where it is known as "television rock." When ulexite forms as masses of parallel fibrous crystals and is cut and polished to about an inch thick, the fibers act as optic pipes to transmit light from below the mineral to the top. A fascinating result is that a newspaper, for example, placed under the mineral can be read on the top of the crystal surface.

Ulexite forms in salt-marsh deposits in arid regions and as bedded sedimentary deposits that form in such environments. It is colorless or white, forming acicular tufts or fibrous masses that look like cotton balls. Crystals are translucent with vitreous luster.

Major ulexite deposits occur in Esmeralda County, Nevada, and Death Valley and Inyo and Kern Counties, California.

Metaphysical associations: revelation of the solution to a problem; knowing the thoughts of others

Commonly found with colemanite, calcite, gypsum, and halite.

VANADINITE

FORMULA: $Pb_5(VO_4)_3Cl$
CLASS: **vanadates**
CRYSTAL SYSTEM: **hexagonal**
HARDNESS: **3**

The name comes from the vanadium content of this mineral. Vanadinite is a rare secondary mineral that forms in the oxidized zones of lead-bearing deposits where vanadium is available from silicates in the wall rock. Its color is bright red to orange with transparent to translucent crystals and vitreous to adamantine luster. Vanadinite typically forms stubby six-sided prisms but can also form rounded masses and crusts.

Arizona produces fine samples from Pima, La Paz, Yuma, Pinal, Cochise, Gila, and Mohave Counties. A yellow arsenic-rich variety, called *endlichite,* occurs in several deposits in New Mexico.

Metaphysical associations: helps one be comfortable in one's own skin; supports not over-spending one's resources; clears the mind of clutter

Commonly found with galena, wulfenite, and cerussite.

VARISCITE

FORMULA: $Al(PO_4) \cdot 2(H_2O)$
CLASS: **phosphates**
CRYSTAL SYSTEM:
orthorhombic
HARDNESS: **4.5**

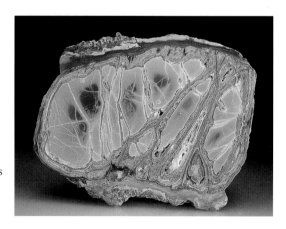

The name of this mineral comes from the word Variscia, an old name for Vogtland, the district in Germany where the mineral was first found. Variscite typically forms from phosphate-bearing waters in contact with aluminous rocks. Variscite is light- to emerald-green in color with a vitreous to waxy luster and translucent crystals. Its typical habit is reniform, massive, or crusts. This mineral is sometimes confused with turquoise, but it is greener and less dense.

Variscite is commonly used as lapidary material. Large nodules occur in Box Elder and Tooele Counties, Utah. Other occurrences include Cochise County, Arizona, and crystallized specimens in Eureka County, Nevada.

Metaphysical associations: gives strength, faith, and tenacity for dealing with great difficulties

Commonly found with apatite and chalcedony.

VESUVIANITE

FORMULA:
$Ca_{10}(Mg,Fe)_2Al_4Si_9O_{34}(OH)_4$
CLASS: silicates
CRYSTAL SYSTEM: tetragonal
HARDNESS: 6.5

This mineral is named for the location at which it was first found—Mt. Vesuvius, Campania, Italy. Vesuvianite forms from the metamorphism of limestones. It is also found in **mafic** and **ultramafic** rocks. Its color is usually green, but it can be brown, yellow, blue, or purple. Its luster is vitreous or greasy, and crystals are transparent to translucent. Its typical habit is short pyramidal to long prismatic crystals but can also be columnar, granular, or massive.

Nice crystals are found throughout the world including in El Dorado and Riverside Counties, California, and Lyon County, Nevada.

Metaphysical associations: dispels anger; promotes cooperation and goodwill

Commonly found with grossular, epidote, and calcite.

WILLEMITE

FORMULA: $Zn_2(SiO_4)$
CLASS: silicates

CRYSTAL SYSTEM: hexagonal
HARDNESS: 5.5

Willemite is named for William I
(1772–1843), King of the Netherlands
(1815–1840). This is a secondary mineral
formed in oxidized zinc deposits. It can be
yellow, red, green, brown, white, or
colorless, with a vitreous luster and
transparent to translucent crystals. It is a
popular mineral among collectors because it
commonly has bright-green fluorescence, a
feature discovered accidentally by a miner
in New Jersey but used thereafter as an
identification tool. However, all willemite is
not fluorescent. Its habit is usually short
prismatic crystals, but willemite can also
form granular or fibrous masses.

Occurrences include Pinal and La Paz Counties, Arizona; Inyo County,
California; and Luna County, New Mexico.

*Metaphysical associations: assists with new beginnings, especially the start of new
spiritual journeys*

Commonly found with malachite, mimetite, and rosasite.

WULFENITE
FORMULA: $Pb(MoO_4)$
CLASS: molybdates
CRYSTAL SYSTEM: tetragonal
HARDNESS: 3

This mineral is named after
Austrian mineralogist Franz
Xaver von Wulfen
(1728–1805). It is a secondary
mineral found in oxidized
portions of lead deposits, and it is quite common throughout Arizona. It is usually
red or orange, but it can be yellow, blue, or colorless. It has vitreous to adamantine

luster with transparent to translucent crystals that form square tablets, often thin or pyramidal.

Some of the highest-quality bright-red, gemmy wulfenite in the world comes from the Red Cloud Mine in Yuma County, Arizona. Other occurrences include La Paz, Pima, Pinal, Santa Cruz, and Cochise Counties, Arizona; Doña Ana County, New Mexico; and Elko County, Nevada.

Metaphysical associations: helps integrate the "shadow" influences and achieve realistic balance of divergent energies; assists in clarifying why specific people are in our lives; useful for white magic

Commonly found with galena, vanadinite, mimetite, and cerussite.

ZEOLITE (GROUP)

FORMULAS: see below
CLASS: silicates
CRYSTAL SYSTEM: varies
HARDNESS: varies

Chabazite

The name for this group of minerals comes from the Greek *zein,* "to boil," and *lithos,* "a stone," because water within the crystal can be driven off when heated. Zeolites are hydrated silicate minerals with **cations** of barium, potassium, sodium, aluminum, cesium, strontium, calcium, or magnesium. Zeolites result from weathering, **devitrification,** or metamorphism of volcanic rocks in low-pressure, low-temperature environments.

Because of the unique crystal structure of zeolite, these minerals have many important uses. One use is as a water softener. Zeolites have the ability

Heulandite

Natrolite

to trade the sodium ions in their structure with the "hard" calcium ions in the water, thus removing the calcium from the water and making it "soft." Similarly, zeolites can filter odors and remove toxins, and act as a chemical sieve. Most municipal water supplies are processed through zeolite before public consumption. Because of their usefulness, zeolites are often synthesized for industrial applications.

Sodalite

Zeolite can be broken down into three different structural variations. One forms needle-like or acicular crystals, as with natrolite; another forms sheets of flattened tabular crystals, as in heulandite; and the third forms equant crystals, as in chabazite. There are about 45 natural minerals that are recognized members of the zeolite group, and they vary in color, luster, and diaphaneity. Some of the better-known zeolites are:

Stilbite (cream) and elbaite (pink)

Chabazite: $CaAl_2Si_4O_{12} \cdot 6(H_2O)$, hexagonal, 4–5 hardness
Heulandite: $CaAl_2Si_7O_{18} \cdot 6(H_2O)$, monoclinic, 3.5–4 hardness
Natrolite: $Na_2Al_2Si_3O_{10} \cdot 2(H_2O)$, orthorhombic, 5–5.5 hardness
Sodalite: $Na_3Al_3Si_3O_{12} \cdot NaCl$, cubic, 5.5–6 hardness
Stilbite: $CaAl_2Si_7O_{18} \cdot 7(H_2O)$, monoclinic, 3.5–4 hardness

Zeolites are mined in Graham and Mohave Counties, Arizona; Sierra County, New Mexico; and San Bernardino and Inyo Counties, California.

Metaphysical associations: absorbs toxins; beneficial to gardens; useful for Reiki
Commonly found with quartz, calcite, and other zeolites.

SOURCES/FOR FURTHER READING

Anthony, John W., Richard A. Bideaux, Kenneth W. Bladh, and Monte C. Nichols. *Handbook of Mineralogy*. Tucson, AZ: Mineral Data Publishing, 1990.

Bahti, Mark. *Spirit in the Stone: A Handbook of Southwest Indian Animal Carvings and Beliefs*. Tucson, AZ: Rio Nuevo Publishing, 1999.

Hall, Judy. *The Crystal Bible: A Definitive Guide to Crystals*. Cincinnati, OH: Walking Stick Press, 2003.

Holden, Martin. *The Encyclopedia of Gemstones and Minerals*, New York: Michael Friedman Publishing Group Inc., 1991.

Knurh, Bruce G. *Gems in Myth, Legend and Lore*. Thornton, CO: Jewelers Press, 1999.

"Melody." *Love Is in the Earth: A Kaleidoscope of Crystals*, updated. Wheat Ridge, CO: Earth-Love Publishing House, 1995.

Perkins, Dexter. *Mineralogy*, 2nd ed. Upper Saddle River, NJ: Prentice Hall, 2001.

USEFUL WEBSITES

http://minerals.usgs.gov/minerals/
http://rruff.geo.arizona.edu/rruff/
http://minsocam.org

GLOSSARY

accessory mineral a mineral present in a rock in small enough amounts to be insignificant in naming or classifying the rock

anion an atom or complex of atoms that has gained one or more electrons and carries a negative charge; a negative ion

cation an atom or complex of atoms that has lost one or more electrons and carries a charge; a postive ion

craton portion of continent that is no longer affected by mountain-building activity; the oldest part of a continent

devitrification the process of changing from glass to crystalline structure

diagenesis chemical, physical, and biological changes undergone by sediment or sedimentary rocks after deposition, not including weathering or metamorphic changes

evaporite mineral a mineral that forms by precipitation from aqueous solution—for example, halite

extrusive rocks type of igneous rocks. Extrusive rocks form on the earth's surface and cool quickly

gangue the uneconomic minerals in an orebody

greisen an altered granitic rock containing mostly quartz, and mica; found as margins along mineral veins or as large bodies at the top and sides of granite intrusions

hydrothermal fluid very hot fluids resulting from igneous activity; can be residual fluids formed during late crystallization of an igneous intrusion or groundwater heated during crystallization of the intrusion

hydrothermal mineral a mineral formed by precipitation from a hydrothermal fluid

igneous a type of rock formed from the cooling of molten material resulting from the partial melting of the earth's crust or mantle

intrusive rocks type of igneous rocks. Intrusive rocks remain below the surface and cool slowly

lithosphere the upper layer of the Earth, comprising the crust and the uppermost mantle

mafic, ultramafic relating to rocks or minerals that are rich in magnesium and iron

magma naturally occurring molten rock resulting from partial melting of the Earth's crust or mantle; the raw material of igneous rocks

magmatism the formation of igneous rocks from magma

mantle the part of the Earth that lies beneath the crust and above the core; the depths vary greatly depending on a number of factors, but on average the mantle begins roughly 22 miles below the surface and ends at a depth of about 1,800 miles

metamorphic rocks or minerals formed as a result of heat and intense pressure but not enough to cause complete melting

ore any rock or mineral that can be mined or worked for a profit

oxidation chemical reaction in which an atom loses electrons

pegmatite an extremely coarse-grained igneous rock usually formed by crystallization of magma enriched in volatiles and trace elements

plates segments of the lithosphere bounded by belts of earthquakes and volcanic activity; these belts are called plate margins

polymorph two or more minerals with the same chemical composition but different crystal structure

porphyry copper deposit a large mineral deposit formed when ascending magma heats groundwater enough to cause it to leach metals from existing rock and circulate it with the moving water; when the water cools, the minerals precipitate, forming large deposits

primary mineral a mineral formed at the same time as the rock in which it is found

schist a well-foliated metamorphic rock characterized by alignment of tabular minerals and grains that are visible with the naked eye

secondary mineral a mineral formed from the alteration of a primary mineral

sedimentary rock or deposit formed from the accumulation of sediments that have been compacted and cemented together

silicification the introduction of cryptocrystalline (smaller than microscopic crystals) silica into a non-siliceous rock or other material (such as a plant) by fluids; the silica fills pore spaces or replaces existing minerals

speleothem a calcium carbonate rock deposited in a cave by precipitation of calcite from water

spreading center an area where two lithospheric plates are moving apart from each other

subduction the process of consumption of a lithospheric plate in which two plates are converging and one is sinking below the other

sublimate a solid substance that has condensed directly from a gas

tectonism movement of lithospheric plates and deformation of crust resulting from processes occurring within the earth

twinning intergrowths of single crystals of the same mineral sharing common atoms; the crystals in **contact twins** meet along a plane; the crystals in **penetration twins** pass through each other

type locality the geographical location where the mineral was first found or described

veins fractures in rocks along which minerals have been deposited

vesicle small cavity in a rock often formed from the presence of gas when cooling

volatile a dissolved element in a silicate magma, such as water or carbon dioxide, which would be a gas at a particular temperature if not for the confining pressure; therefore, when pressure is released, such as when magma rises to the earth's surface, the volatiles enter into the gas phase

INDEX

*(NOTE: terms in **boldface** denote names of specific minerals featured in this book)*